MW00878700

GOD TALKS

Supernatural Manifestations of
God's Guidance through God Talks

By SABRINA C. LEWIS

PRESS

GOD TALKS
Supernatural Manifestations of God's Guidance through God Talks
by Sabrina C. Lewis

Printed in the United States of America.
Edited by Xulon Press

ISBN 9781498445559

www.xulonpress.com

Dedication

This book is dedicated in the memory of:

Mother Bernice Hart
Mother Marie Washington
Sister Callie Mae Lewis
Bro. Bobby Seagers
Deacon Royce Williams
Sister Thelma Griffin
Elder Edward Williams

Table of Contents

Acknowledgments

I give honor to God the Father, His Son, Jesus, and to the Holy Spirit for every "God Talk." I would like to thank with much appreciation my family, friends, the Heart of Jesus Church family, Carpentersville Baptist Church family and a special thanks to my dear friend Linda Johnson. Everyone's comments and friendships were of enormous value to me in the writing process of the book.

Preface

We cannot discount these mysterious occurrences, although we may not be able to explain them. For we have all had them at some time or another, although for so long it has been unconscionable to speak of such things in our traditional church settings and many have suppressed or ignored them, casting them off as just figments of the imagination. Privately, people will admit that these encounters were much more and they cannot shake them, but they are ever there, buried deeply in the core of their being. Religious rigidity doesn't give way to such sharing. Why, one might be perceived as a deviant and risk ostracism from the status quo. Would you, my friend, "Give Place" to talking to God about these instances? Perhaps there was a time God brought you to the end of your own strength and became strength for you. There is an invitation extended through these mysterious encounters, where God unveils Himself through revelations of His Son, Jesus Christ, whereby we have access to "treasures of darkness and hidden riches" (Isaiah 45:3) of the deep things of God, and they are made plain through "God Talks."

You might have pursued Him as you caught a glimpse of Him. Your brief encounter was enough to arouse a hunger in your spirit and knowledge that there is something more. There is a burden in your spirit for the supernatural and beyond the traditional religious settings. You hunger for so much more. You can't deny the witness of your spirit — your awareness that God has designed and orchestrated everything that touches our lives to bring us all into oneness with Him through the knowledge of His Son, Jesus. In attempts to explain this phenomenon, man is ever in pursuit of a closer relationship with God. There is a domain beyond the senses: it is called faith. Faith in and of itself leads us to "God Talks." An ever relentless desire compels us to know that there is something from beyond what we might otherwise be able to explain in the limited confines of language when we have "God Talks." Nature itself sends out invitations through the vastness of its complexities that even the most ingenious mind cannot fathom: Awe and Thrills. People might find out that they are on the brink of totally abandoning themselves to nature. If they would just accept the inevitable "God Talks." He is talking to you through the very pages of this book, at this very moment. You hear Him talking: Just talk back in the earnestness of your innermost being and relish the moments, for He is much obliged to have "God Talks" with you.

Introduction

M y most transforming life experiences have been as a result of "God Talks." Everything else pales in comparison to talking with God and having God talk to you. Throughout my whole life, I have had such wonderful experiences that I am compelled to write about them.

I know "God Talks" saved my life and steered me along the rugged path. I would have been doomed without them, and I know with surety that He wants me to share these moments with others.

One of the most influential people God placed in my life was Eliza Mathis, my grandmother — affectionately known as "Momma." My mom left me in her care along with my other siblings when I was just six years old. I can still hear her talking with God. I now believe that's how He graciously taught me the value of "God Talks." It was her voice that pierced the darkness of the night and brought rays of hope to my traumatic childhood. Momma would talk to God all night. Those moments were sacred to her. Many nights, I would call out to her, only to hear her respond, "Hush gal, don't you hear me talking with the Lord?" Somewhere along the way, I started doing the same, and I have been having "God Talks" ever since.

It is time for the nations to have "God Talks." If we begin to have "God Talks," we will hear God talk. He wants to have a "God Talk" with us. We don't need to concern ourselves with the logistics. All we need to do is have a "God Talk." Religion has often impeded us from having "God Talks," and religion has often impeded us from unity with God. God has never been bound by religion. People have just thought they had Him bound through religion. I am here to announce to the nations that He is running the show and I heard Him say: "It is Show Time!" God is about to show Himself throughout the nations, and those who are having "God Talks" will redeem the time and have discernment for the ages. The Lord is saying to those who have said, "The vision is for many days to come and the times are far off, that none of His Words shall be prolonged any more, but the Word that He spoke shall be done." (Ezekiel 12:26-28).

It is not in a method, but in faith that we apprehend Him. He is captured; simply taken by our approaching Him. This is the moment He has been awaiting, for us to come to Him. When we start having "God Talks," He will direct us in such a way that the consummation of all things will truly be manifested. Our acknowledgement of Him will bring revelations of Him and of ourselves as never before seen under the heavens. So, let's have "God Talks."

Chapter One

Highway to Destiny

"God Talks"

"And we know that all things work together
for good to them that love God, and are called
according to His purpose."
~ Romans 8:28

My Journey Begins

I was thrust into a state of consciousness, emerging into the world as if someone had sketched me into a scene. I was animated, alive and aware. I was just a small child, about four or five. (I honestly can't recall, but I am certain that I was one or the other.) For me, that is where life began. Life seemed to come in bits and pieces, but these bits and pieces were the groundwork of much greater experiences, all of which brought me to "God Talks."

I was aware from the beginning that I was in and a part of something great — Life. I examined my surroundings, but I had nothing to reference this place of consciousness to; that is what I would like to call it for now. I was also keenly aware that I had come from some place … and that there was no returning – at least for the time being … and I had no choice in the matter.

My eyes were stretched wide-open. Somehow, I was trying to take it all in, but before I could absorb this state of consciousness, things started happening at the speed of light. I didn't have time to catch my breath. It was as if someone in the great heavens said – Action! — and there I was. I heard a noise in our house. Two men jumped from behind the door. Oh my God, they were fighting my daddy. I was paralyzed; nothing moved in me, my heart was about to jump out of my chest.

"Stop it. Stop it!"

My daddy was badly hurt. It appeared as if there was no one else home, but my daddy, his attackers and me. I vaguely remember hearing some of the grown-ups saying my mom's boyfriend attacked my daddy and almost killed him. All I remember is the scene quickly changed and we were no longer in our little house together as a family, but in the Projects of Miami with just our mom.

It was dark and the stench of urine filled the room. Sweaty, tiny-little bodies lay motionless on the mattresses of the bunk beds. The moisture was digging sores into my raw skin and the wetness was stinging me. I tried to open the door of the room, but it was locked. I felt as if I might suffocate.

"Mom, let us out." I beat and banged helplessly on the door, but to no avail. She was gone as usual. I should have known. After all, it was the routine: she would pour almost a whole gallon of Clorox into the tub of water in the bathroom, bathe us, and then lock us back in the dark room. I was almost suffocating. I couldn't tell my sweat from my tears as they mingled together. I had to get my brothers and sisters some help. Beams of light flooded the room at night from a lamp-pole outside. It was just enough light for me to know there was a way out.

There was the sound of grunting and slight whining. My siblings were waking up. I felt so empty inside. I was so hungry. Almost faint, I made it to the only window in the room. I pressed my malnourished frame against it while feeling for the latch. At five years old, I was the oldest of the group. My brother, Rodney was four, Michele was three, and Paula and Paul were around one. I tried to console my siblings. "I am going to get help." I managed to open the window and climbed out into more darkness.

I went around to the front of the apartment building to the lady who lived in front of us. I desperately banged on her door. As always, she let her oldest daughter come help us. I don't even remember their names, but I could never forget their acts of kindness. No matter how many times I went, they would help us. I am sure now it was only the goodness of God. The neighbor's daughter would climb through the window and pry the room door open and stay with us until my mom came back.

I never understood my mom's behavior. I now know that her behavior was far from normal and that she must have suffered from some form of undiagnosed mental illness. How else could I explain her behavior? She was beautiful, and as a child she could do no wrong in my eyes. I completely adored her. As I wrote this, I was about to say she never physically abused us, but then the memories of the Clorox brought tears to my eyes — that was abuse in itself. I am still trying to compensate for it. I just remember clinging to her whenever she was around. I wanted so much to be with her.

The smell of mildew, a sour smell, always filled the living room, dining room and kitchen in our Project housing. My mom would let the food spoil rather than feed us. Many days I would climb out the window, taking only my brother, Rodney, and sneak to the park during the summer to go to the "Feed A Kid" program. I would always have to beg for my other sisters and brother, and somehow God would always grant me the favor; they would give me the extra meals. They probably had no clue that this would be the only food we would get. When the season for "Feed A Kid" ended, it was just the grace of God that we didn't starve to death.

I don't ever recall Mom feeding us. A few times I remember she took us off with her, but that only happened every now and then. The only things I recall as not being spoiled in the refrigerator were a few Mr. GoodBars, but we knew not to touch them. My siblings and I were all bellies and bones. Our heads seemed disproportionate to our bodies; the only thing big on us was our heads.

Mr. GoodBar

Every now and then, Mom's boyfriend's brother would babysit us. He was real dark-skinned and he smelled funny. When he would babysit us, he would sometimes get us out of the room. He really took a liking to me and treated me somewhat differently than my siblings. I don't remember his name, but I do remember how he would play with me. He would touch me. He would lay me on the floor and get on top of me. He was big and the weight from his body would press me into the cold cement floor and he would wiggle and wiggle. I couldn't breathe.

"What are you doing?" I don't recall him giving me an answer, but afterward he would give my siblings and me our mom's Mr. GoodBars. He promised as long as I would never tell, he would always give us Mr. GoodBars.

One day we were playing and he asked me to take my clothes off. He had never asked me to do that before, and the only time I could associate with taking my clothes off was where my mom would pile all of us in the tiny Clorox tub. I remember crying and asking if it was bath time. He said, "No." I will never know, but I am sure as I look back, God was sparing me from further physical violations. I started crying uncontrollably. He tried helplessly to stop me, but he couldn't calm me. He became angry and shoved me back in the room with my siblings and locked the door. I remember, I just couldn't stop crying, and even now I don't know why. At the moment, as much as I loved the Mr. GoodBars, even that was not enough incentive for me to stop crying.

When my mom got home much later that night, I was still crying. He didn't tarry when she got home, but quickly left. She let us out of the room and we were sitting in the living room but I was still crying, and for the first time she seemed to show some concern for me. She turned to me and asked me what was wrong. The only words that made it out of my mouth were, "He wanted me to take my clothes off." My mom didn't give me time to finish, it was as if she knew what had happened and she left the house in a rage.

The next day around the Project, there was talk of a man being shot in the back. I could only believe that had something to do with my mom, but it wasn't until I was grown and inquired about it that I knew for sure. My mom told me she meant to kill him.

My mom brought a baby home. Funny, I don't recall her being pregnant, or maybe I just didn't know what that was. After all, it wasn't like my mom talked to us, or even that we saw much of her, but one day she came in with a baby. I thought she went to a baby store and picked the baby out. She was beautiful: she was my new little sister. The new baby didn't change things for us; it only meant I had another sibling to look after. I had come to a place where my sisters and brothers felt more like my children than my siblings. Instead of playing house, I was a child running a house by instincts of survival that I now know God had woven into me.

When I was not at home, I remember going to school in a trailer not far from the Project housing. I was in kindergarten, but that's about all I remember. I remember first grade a lot better. My mom would make sure she fixed me up well for school. My mom would straighten my hair with Crisco Oil. I could still feel the heat on my scalp, not to mention how I smelled like Crisco. I was always worried about my babies and what was happening to them when I had to go to school.

I heard a lot about Watergate on television when my mom occasionally got us out of the dark room and we sat around in the living room with her. It seemed frightening to me. I wondered what all the commotion was about. I envisioned it was some big gate with water behind it, and we were all going to drown when it burst. I later learned when I had grown up that it was related to politics. It felt good not to be locked up in the room.

I finally saw my daddy again. It seemed like an eternity since I had seen him last. He wasn't hurt anymore. He came by my school and was waiting at the gate for me. I loved my daddy. I got in the car with him, and he asked me about my brothers and sisters. He told me that I couldn't tell my mom about our visit, and I never did. He often would come by, and sometimes he would give me money. I always felt special with my daddy, and I knew my daddy loved me. I knew something bad was going on between my mom and daddy. I later would learn they were in a nasty divorce, and my daddy couldn't come to our house.

Just when I got a glimmer of hope with school, another babysitter experience would further add insult to injury. This man lived in the Projects, and apparently others trusted him with their children also. I didn't feel comfortable from the first time my mom left us with him. He was a big, fat, dark-skinned guy, and he looked like he weighed a few hundred pounds. He would ask if we wanted to play "Ring Around the Roses." I don't know why he would ask, because it did not matter what we wanted. He would tell us all to get in a circle and join hands. Then he would go around the circle from child to child, assaulting us in ways you could never imagine. He would laugh as he went around the circle. I hated when he got to my siblings and me. Everyone would be crying. I remembered I couldn't breathe. I felt like I was choking. I remember gagging and spitting. My mouth felt funny — so funny. "Somebody, please help us." I cried desperately in my mind. No one said anything. No one ever said anything. In fact, I never told my mom.

Every now and then, God would send my Aunt Evelyn to rescue us. She would pick us up and take us with her to Jay's my mom's first cousin who my Aunt Evelyn lived with. She knew some things about what my mom was doing, but she never talked to us about it. It just never came up. She was so good to us. She would feed us and bathe us and she didn't put Clorox in the water. In fact, taking a bath at her house was pleasant. Of course, the time would come that we would have to go home to be locked up in the room, but for a minute I felt like I could breathe.

My siblings and I were caught in a "Tug of War" between our parents. We finally got to go with my daddy to where he was staying. I remember he had a girlfriend who later became my stepmother. I thought we were going to stay with Daddy, but he brought us to Georgia to his parents' house, my grandparents. This was my first trip to Georgia. Daddy didn't stay; he left. I had to take care of my siblings. I was the momma and they had better behave. My grandmother often told me I was like an old lady. Little did she know, I was! I had experienced so much grown-up stuff, it was difficult for me to be a child.

We were not at my grandma's house long. I certainly enjoyed eating grits every day. There were hogs, chickens, pathways through the woods, cats, cousins, and a little corner store. There was freedom in the wide-open country. Then one day, my mom came with some man name Rufus to take us shopping for shoes. At least, that was the story she told my daddy's mom, but she kept going, straight back to Miami. There we were, back to the room.

Shifting Gears

One day, my mom packed all of our things. She had never done this before. She said we were going to Georgia. I can still remember the car, a Chevrolet, the long road and the night travel. She brought us home to her momma's house. This would be life-changing for me. I didn't know at the time, but God was shifting gears in my life, and placement with my grandmother would introduce me to "God Talks."

We arrived at a little white block house that all but sat on the railroad track in front of it, and 106 10th Street, Waynesboro, Georgia, became my new address.

There was an older lady who came bursting through the wooden screen door onto the porch. She looked over-joyed to see us. She wore an apron tied around her waist and dark shades. I couldn't see her eyes. My mom called her "Momma." Momma was my grandmother and I called her "momma" too. Others came out with her and everybody was hugging. I quickly became preoccupied with the scent of food. I just wanted to get in Momma's house to the food. The door opened and we followed her to the kitchen.

She asked, "Yawl chillen hungry?" Hungry wasn't the word, I felt like I hadn't eaten since my last visit to Georgia, which was over a year ago.

Momma's stove was covered with food. It looked like paradise to me. Fried chicken looked like it reached to the ceiling, corn bread, macaroni and cheese, some kind of beans. I started grabbing fried chicken and shoving it down as quickly as I could. For the first time in my six years, I felt full. I ate and ate and ate.

I knew from that moment on, this was the place to be. That is, until I heard the most terrifying sound I ever heard in my life: the sound of the train's whistle. The train sounded like it was coming into the house. I screamed and covered my ears with my hands to stop the sound, but my hands were no match for that whistle; it went straight through my head. I took off running, the old wooden screen door slamming behind me. I ran as fast as I could to the back yard, as far as I could go. Then I caught a glimpse of it, the huge black train with its two big, round eyes that were close together. It was some kind of monster and it had come to get me. I was pow-erless and the only place I felt safe was as far as I could get away from it. It soon passed by, but it took a moment before I would get my composure and go back to the front of the house. Since this was to become my new home for now, I was certain that the train and I would always be in conflict.

The scenes of life slowed down a little, and for the first time in my few years the pace had slowed just enough for me to gather more impressions from the journey. This conflict with the train would definitely be a long haul for me. I had to always be on the lookout because it had a way of popping up on me, so I had to learn to react quickly whenever I heard the faintest sound of the whistle. I even formed a very close relationship with an old man in my new neighborhood name Mr. John. He always told me how special I was and he always gave me nickels and quarters. He told the day would come when I would understand what he meant by calling me a special child but he warned me he might be dead and gone by the time I would understand. He told me no matter what don't forget that I am special and in time I would know. Mr. John was so very dear to me.

My siblings and I were very malnourished, but now we were in the best place ever, in the care of my grandparents, Eliza and Boozie Mathis. Momma would surely nurture us, along with my older cousins: Brenda, Karen, Liz, Willie Earnest and Lloyd. I know they noticed how strange we were. I remember sitting in the living room with my siblings. As we sat on the couch, we would rock backward and forward and bump our heads against the back of the couch and make strange noises — like humming sounds. We would also rock in our sleep. I didn't know why then, but I now know we were engaging in self-stimulatory behavior. To us, I believe it was some form of comfort. I remember we all wet the bed. Well, I didn't wet the bed until we got to Georgia. What I didn't understand at that time was the trauma of all that we had been through led to a regression in all of us, but seemingly especially me. I knew we were odd because our cousins didn't act like us.

All this brought me to "God Talks," or maybe it was what God did so He could bring me to a place where He could talk to me. One thing for sure, this had all been a whirlwind of a ride and no one understood me. Honestly, I didn't understand me. I was just trying to get a grip on things. To sum things up, I was confused, belligerent, and traumatized. Here I was, whether or not I wanted to be here at all — whether I understood it or not. Nobody asked me anything. I was enrolled in a new school. My mom disappeared without any word to me while I was at school. I had to adjust to a strange place with people I really didn't know well — except for my Aunt Evelyn, who had rescued my siblings and me occasionally when we were in Florida. I can't remember how she came to Georgia, but she was at Momma's house. In fact, my cousins were her children. When I was in Florida and she would come to get us, there were no children there. It turned out that my grandma was raising my Aunt Evelyn's children. If I can recall correctly, she had come to get a place and move her children to be with her, but that would take a while. For now, we were all at Momma's house. Sometimes we would take turns flip flopping; some staying at Momma's house and some staying at Daddy Boozie's house, down the street across the railroad track.

One day, Momma said she could no longer keep all of us because there were too many of us. She said her "head had bloomed for the grave." So she said she would have to send the smaller ones back to my mom. I didn't really understand what all that meant, but one day they packed up my babies and sent them away. We were split apart, and for the first time in our lives separated. My Aunt Evelyn took Michelle, Paula and Paul back to Miami, and only Rodney, my baby sister Veronica and I were left in Georgia. If that wasn't enough, my other aunt, who lived in Georgia, took my baby sister to live with her.

This was more than I could bear, and my heart felt like someone ripped it out without an apology. Too much, too fast, not enough time to catch my breath. No, not even a moment to sigh. Despair anchored itself in my heart and later turned to rage, and all I had left was Rodney. All I could think about was who would take care of my little sisters and brother who up until this time only knew me – a six-year-old mother. What could I do? I got over it, but certainly not without some serious pitfalls.

Momma was always talking to God. I often heard her through the night and many days, especially after my Aunt Evelyn moved out and took my cousins. Momma and I would sit on the front porch talking to the Lord. She would sit on the old metal chair next to the glider and I would sit in my rocking chair on the end of the porch. These were times of healing. I could rock and rock, back and forth, as if to rock all my troubles away. Momma would have "God Talks" and I started having "God Talks." She often told me, "The Lord hears prayers." I spent years rocking and years praying. I would plead with the Lord to let my mom come home. All my "God Talks" were about my mom. I prayed from the time I was six years old until I was thirteen years old for my mom to come home. She only came to Georgia twice since she left us with Momma, and that was when she went to jail and when she came to Daddy Boozie's funeral.

She came and she left. From that point on, she spent years promising to come home, but she never kept her promises. Holidays passed, birthdays passed, years passed. I had "God Talks" faithfully every day for my mom. I would sit on the porch in my rocking chair, often gazing up in the top of the huge pecan trees in hundred-degree temperatures and then through the frigid winter temperatures. I felt no obstacle kept me from having "God Talks" for my mom. One thing for sure, I was persistent and diligent in having my "God Talks." I expected He would one day "Talk."

She is Not Coming Home

After many years, from the time I was six years old to thirteen years old, "God Talked." Well, He talked a lot during those years, but those talks are reflected in other "God Talks." This particular "God Talk" was directly related to my request for my mom to come home, which had been my cry for the past seven years. I was sitting on the front porch as always and "God Talked." When "God Talks," He is straight to the point and He doesn't beat around the bush. He was blunt with me, and I can only believe in His mercy that He didn't answer me sooner; perhaps because He was waiting for me to grow to a place that I could receive the answer. I am certain He always knew the answer. He didn't tell me until I was thirteen. I believe God was having me develop a relationship with Him along the way. Nevertheless, the day came and "God Talked."

He said, "She is not coming home." Before that could sink into my heart, God knew my thoughts afar off, so He gave clarity. He said, "In fact, she will never put her feet in Georgia again."

Receiving such news after praying so long wasn't upsetting at all. It was like relief. It was like I could get over it and live. Every tear I ever cried for my mom seemed to dry up. My soul was no longer hemorrhaging. I called my mom that evening, and for all the times she misled me and said it wasn't her and hung up the phone or said, "Barbara isn't home," God allowed her to answer the phone and acknowledge it was her. When she did, I told her how it didn't matter anymore, and that she didn't have to call anymore. Especially, she didn't have to call my grandma, the only person my brother and I had now, and break her heart over and over with disappointment. I told my mom, "Just don't call." I hung the phone up, ready for a fresh start.

Whatever God says, it will come to pass. I didn't see my mom again until I was eighteen, and when I did, she didn't know who I was. It was like a dream. She wanted me to sit in her lap. She wanted to hold me close, and after so many years, I still desired to be close to her. For a brief moment, I thought maybe this would be a new beginning for the two of us, but it only lasted a moment like the blink of an eye. She had proved to me that old habits die hard. She promised the next day we would get together again, but some things never change. The next day she dodged us. She didn't show up.

Then ten years later, my mom started calling me. I had always maintained that you can't miss what you never had. I toughened my skin and maintained an indifference concerning my mom. That was the best way to avoid the pain. She would call, and I convinced myself I really did not have much to talk about with her. She was like a stranger. What do you talk about with someone you don't know? A part of me wanted to be stubborn. A part of me wanted to cave in, but I chose not to be needy. So I acted like I was distant and didn't want to talk when she called.

Then one day my daddy called, very concerned and almost with urgency in his voice. He said, "You need to come to Miami and see your mom: She is very ill." Then he said those dreaded words: "She has cancer."

It was as if a switch clicked on in my head and it became apparent, "That's why she had been calling." She had never called before, and now suddenly she was calling. I wanted to believe she was sincere. I was all the more convinced that it was because she needed me now. The words that my Aunt Kin would so often say to me rang in my ears with the pitch of an ambulance siren. I remembered when I was a little girl, how I would overhear Aunt Kin in conversation with my grandma, saying my mom had called, and I would ask whether or not my mom asked about my brother and me.

My aunt would hesitate, not wanting to disclose the awful truth: "Baby, she didn't even mention y'all name." Then she would bend down and look me in the eyes and say, "One day before Bobbie leaves this world, you are going to have to bathe her."

I didn't understand what my aunt was saying at the time and it was of little consolation when I was small. Now thoughts were swirling in my head. It was all so clear. The pain roused and lodged in my chest and throat. At that moment, air eluded me and I gasped for a breath. "I don't owe her nothing," I protested, as if to convince myself, as if I believed it. All my life, I had always maintained, since the "God Talk" that revealed my mom would never come home again, that I would always go aide her should she ever need me. I always said that just because she wasn't there for me would not keep me from doing all I could for her, because I loved her. Now the moment of truth was upon me and I had such mixed emotions. Perhaps I had not forgiven her as I had believed. Why would I be so torn, so hurt?

When I returned to work that Monday, I shared the news about my mom with my co-workers. They had often heard my story and always offered support. One of my co-workers grew up with my mom in Burke County, and would often ask about her. She knew how my mom abandoned all nine of her children. For years I knew nothing of my older sister Debbie and my older brother Joe Jr. and then my mom had another daughter after my sister Veronica. Her name was Vershawn and she ended up being raised by a foster parent. So my mom gave birth to nine children in all. She advised me that whatever I chose to do, not to let my mom leave this world without finding out why she did what she did to us. In my mind, I didn't know whether that was so important to me. It wasn't until the end of my workday, as I was driving down Tobacco Road in Augusta, Ga., that I cried out sobbing uncontrollably during a "God Talk" and made a confession.

"Oh God, it is a lie, when someone says you can't miss what you never had. You can miss what you had always hoped to have had, and when the person is gone, even the hope of what you could have is gone." I could not gather my composure. So I pulled off to the side of the road. The Spirit of the Lord consoled me, forgiveness flooded my heart, and I knew what I had to do. I had to make haste to get to my mom.

She is All Right

I left the next day with what little money I had, my baby, and a good friend of mine, Julie. She agreed to go with me on the spur of a moment, when it looked like my baby and I would be traveling alone. This was the first time I ever drove to Miami. In fact, it was the first time I ever drove a long distance.

I had many "God Talks" by this time, but one in particular during this season encouraged me concerning my mom. It was one Tuesday night, while in prayer service having a "God Talk," God said to me concerning my mom, "It is all right." That was all He said, but that was enough. People were so generous to help me, especially my co-workers at Gracewood State School and Hospital. Pastor Herman Bing, my dear friend in the Lord and spiritual father in ministry, took up over $900 for me. There were no words for such generosity.

When I got to Miami, my sister, Paula was helping my mom as much as she could. She became my helper as well when I arrived in Miami. I didn't know my way around Miami, so she was my guide during my stay. She took me to my mom's place. When we got to the apartment and knocked on the door, my mom answered. She opened the door, a thin, frail frame ravaged by cancer. Her voice was almost faint, but she had a smile that glowed in awe at her unexpected guest, and it revealed all that I needed and more. For the first time in my life, after ten years since last I saw her, I perceived my mom was glad to see me.

I was euphoric when my mom opened her arms, which appeared elongated because they were so thin, and graciously lavished me with a long-awaited hug. Oh, the joy that flooded my soul. My mom. All I wanted to do was love on her. She didn't owe me anything. All I wanted to do was lavish her with love and serve her in any way I could. She looked down at the little toddler at my side and said, "Rockriegus." Funny, she couldn't pronounce my son's name, "Rardietrick," but what did it matter? We were in each other's presence, granted an opportunity perhaps to get to know each other. God ordained this trip.

It would be one of two trips that I would make before her death. I went back to Miami a month later. This time, my Aunt Kin and I traveled together. My mom's state had worsened from my first visit. She didn't want us out of her presence. She seemed enlivened by our being with her. Every word God spoke would come to pass. His Word may tarry but will not fail. I bathed my mom. I helped her in the tub, and my two-year-old baby and I washed her back. It was just as my aunt had so often said, "Before, Bobbie leaves this earth, you are going to have to bathe her." My eyes flooded with tears. I couldn't hold them back. I concealed my tears lest my mom inquire for what reason I cried. There was a joy, unspeakable and full of glory, that God had granted me such a privilege to serve her. He had given us this moment, and even when death would come, it could not take this from me. She grew increasingly frail and the only thing that mattered to me was that my mom should make a decision for Jesus Christ. I desired to see her saved — nothing else mattered.

When the time came that we should depart, I offered to stay and take a leave of absence from my job, but my daddy and sister insisted that I should go home. Everything would be fine, they assured me. I reluctantly left. I so loved my mom. She was beautiful even sick. She had such a glow about her. Her skin cleared up and it looked so plump and lush, as if it

29

would burst for ripeness. She was resting. We shared what would become our last kiss.

My mom died two months later. I cried. A part of me was hoping for more, but I understood God had rewarded my diligence in prayer. It is written in the word of God how He rewards those who diligently seek Him. My mom had gone on to be with the Lord. The Lord who is rich in mercy had pardoned her and saved her. My "God Talks" once again proved "God Talks." He doesn't always answer us in the way we expect, but He is faithful to His word. "It was all right."

We all came to Florida for her memorial. She had requested to be cremated and that her ashes be scattered in the ocean. I never saw my mom dead. The only memories were of her living. My sister, Debbie had everything taken care of when we got to Miami. I only ached inside for one of my younger sisters, because she strongly desired to see our mom's remains. I knew she needed closure, but it was too late. Closure would have to come for her through some other avenue. We had a small memorial service. My daddy eulogized my mom, and the Lord gave space so that I was able to share some words of comfort with my family. All I could say was what God said to me in my "God Talk." I told my family, "It is all right." Some way, I knew when God said it was all right, it was. I had no further questions and needed no further explanation.

When we arrived at the pier with my mom's ashes in a little wooden box to scatter them, they were still warm to the touch. We each took some in our hands and threw them out into the ocean. We were letting go. Then we cast the little wooden box out in the ocean, and a single rose. For a minute, the little box appeared to linger, and then the current began to carry it out into the ocean, rising and falling with the waves. My mom so loved the water. That was it, the end of a hope and the beginning of memories, a time and a season "God Talked." He reminded me of words He had spoken to me when I was thirteen years old and now here I was, twenty-eight years old. She would never come home again; in fact, she would never put her feet in Georgia again.

It all reminded me of a book by Thomas Wolfe that I read in high school: *You Can't Go Home Again.* Ah, how painfully true! God meant it, so despite my grandma's desire for us to bring her ashes back for burial, providence worked so that not even her ashes could be brought back to Georgia. So there it stood, a "God Talk" fulfilled.

Chapter Two

Prophetic Intersections

"God Talks"

"And He lighted upon a certain place, and tarried
there all night, because the sun was set; and He took
of the stones of that place, and put them for His pillows,
and lay down in that place to sleep."
~ Genesis 28:11

Make the Water Low

I t was revival time at Watkinsville Baptist Church. It was always the second week in August, coming up to the third Sunday. I was seven years old. We just had the Church Anniversary in July, where all the families prepared what I heard Momma called "Boxes." Everybody's trunks were filled with food. This was the best time ever. I would go from trunk to trunk, from family to family, getting as much food as I could. Now that I look back, I don't know how all that food didn't spoil in the dead heat of the summer, but it didn't. I couldn't wait for church to dismiss. The anticipation of eating all that food blocked all else, sermon and all.

Those were the good ole days. Yes, indeed. We would run and play all over the church grounds, all through the graveyard. My great-grandma was buried out there with a host of other relatives. Momma would explain why her mom, "Momma Tina's" grave didn't have a cement top. She said Momma Tina would say, "Don't y'all chillum put no cement on me, when the Lord come, I don't want nothing holding me down." I was always fascinated with the huge trees that towered over the graveyard, keeping the scorching sun at bay. All I knew was this revival was the time for me to get baptized. My cousin, Karen said she was going to do it. Karen was almost two years older than me, but I thought I was just as old as she was.

Everybody knew if you were going to get baptized, there would be a call for you to come and sit on the "Mourning Bench." All you could hear was the sound of feet patting on the wooden floor, fans flapping back and forth as the people fought off the heat. The sounds of humming and mourning filled and bounced off those old wooden walls. All of a sudden, Aunt Pearlie looked like she was boxing as she was singing in the choir stand: "Everybody Ought To Call Him by His Name."

Then as always, every third Sunday she would fall back and scream out, "OOH." I could remember Momma's disapproving expressions, although I could not see her eyes, because everywhere she went including church she always wore dark shades. She would later tell us when we got out of church, "Gee Me-Almighty, Mood carried on a scandalous and a shame." Karen and I would laugh throughout the whole church service sometimes, at the way everybody was getting the "Holy Ghost." Then came the time they called us to the front of the church. Some of the old deacons said a few words and then Rev. Dixon, the pastor, stood over us like a giant and said something to the effect of asking if we were candidates for baptism. Then we took our place. I don't remember what I was thinking, but I realized this was serious. Honestly, I didn't understand what this was all about other than this was what you were supposed to do. Everybody gave their approval, nodding their heads as we took our places. We knelt down and talked to God. I don't remember what I said, but I know we were kneeling for a long time, then they gave us the cue to get up.

One of the deacons gave the cue that the water was ready. We all went outside to the baptism pool. Everybody gathered around and began to sing. Reverend Dixon got down in the old white block cement pool. I could hardly see for all the people, but Karen went in. He put his big hands over Karen's face, said a few words and threw her back under the water and brought her back up. Then it was my turn. I stepped on the first step to go down in the pool. As I made each step, it looked like I never would reach the last one, and by the time I did the water was seeping into my mouth. It was either fight or flight, so I opted for flight and leaped like a squirrel, screaming and hollering way up in Reverend Dixon's arms. I was clinging to him for my life and I wasn't about to let go. Everyone was looking at me and they were saying things, but at the time it didn't matter. As soon as Reverend Dixon put me on the ground, I felt the weight of pocketbooks hitting me. I was under attack. A mob of old ladies were beating me and calling me a devil. I couldn't see Momma, but I squirmed my way through until I could feel some air and then I took off running. They would have to catch me if they could, but I was not letting up until I was far out of their reach. Momma was upset with me to. I think I embarrassed my whole family.

This would all lead to a "God Talk." In fact, it was one of my significant first ones. Revival time came back around again, and this time I couldn't suffer another humiliating moment as I had done previously. In fact, I was the talk of the church for some time "That gal of Liza's." People still looked at me funny. I even believed that perhaps my not getting baptized had something to do with my having to go to summer school so I wouldn't be retained in the third grade.

The churchyard was covered with cars. I couldn't endure a repeat from last year. So, I stole away from everyone when we got to church and went out to the old pump house out in the graveyard to have a "God Talk." I told God, "I really want to get baptized this year, but if the water is high again, I just can't. God, please make the water low this year so those old ladies don't beat me again." It was the sincere cry of a child. I rushed back so no one would miss me. Then I went in and took my seat on the "Mourning Bench," where I had sat all week.

As always, the church rocked with a harmony that seemed to come from heaven itself. I knew that this was the night. I wasn't afraid at all. Soon I saw Deacon Patterson leave and then shortly he returned. He whispered to another deacon to get Reverend Dixon. I was attentively watching their every move. Then I overheard Deacon Patterson ask, "Who turned the water off?" No one in the huddle knew. They all looked confused. Then the question was asked whether or not there was enough water to baptize the candidates. Then, the answer came, "Yes." So the call came for everyone to come outside to the baptism pool. As always everyone gathered around and started singing.

One by one the candidates went forward and then came my turn. I wasn't afraid at all, but I could feel the eyes of the people watching me. I stepped on the first step to go down into the pool. This time as I continued step by step, I noticed in sheer joy that the water was very low. It barely came to my knees. Oh, how my "God Talk" had paid off. I had talked to Him and now He was talking back to me. I knew who had turned the water off. It was God Himself. I stepped on down and turned my back against Reverend Dixon. He covered my whole face with his big hand and then stretched his other hand toward heaven and said a few words. The next thing I knew, he threw me back into the water. I went all the way under and before I could even think another thought, he brought me back up. It was official: I was baptized. All the people around the pool congratulated me. Some even gave me money. I was so excited. This time, I ran through the crowd, not because they were beating me, but I had to go tell God. I knew He saw me. I just wanted to get back out to that old pump house out in the graveyard to have a "God Talk." So, off I went, the full moon lighting the path. I told God, "Thank You for turning the water off. None of the church members knew how the water got turned off. They all had much conversation about that night. They never knew what I knew: It was God.

37

You Must Go On Without Mother, Without Father

The first time I heard the voice of God, I was eight years old. I was in a crisis. The school system misjudged me. Instead of accurately assessing me and coming to the correct conclusion, they apparently thought I had some learning disability or assumed I was disturbed. Although my behaviors were quite odd, I was not dumb by a long shot. After all, even my mom told Momma that the school had to be wrong because I didn't have any problems in school in Miami. My mom told Momma that I was an "A" student. All I knew was that nobody understood my pain, even though I was displaying it the only way I knew. I wasn't throwing desks over in the middle of class just for the fun of it. I wasn't banging on the piano in the middle of class just for the fun of it. I wasn't getting paddled by the principal just about every day for the fun of it. I was crying out for help.

The only person who tried to relate to me and really went out of her way to help me was my third grade teacher, Mrs. Vera Moore. I just want to pause now and tell her how much her genuine concern meant. She would bring me home so many days and tried tirelessly to help me. I don't think I could explain the pain to her, but I believe she saw past all the drama and recognized somewhere inside of me was a scared little girl who just needed so desperately for somebody to hear her cry. Thank you, Mrs. Moore. God gave you to me at this very critical junction.

Long story short, they were going to retain me in the third grade. I had to attend summer school. I was walking across Waynesboro Elementary School yard during summer school, when "God Talked." It would be the first time He talked to me audibly. I heard Him say, "You must go on without mother and without father." As I am writing of this "God Talk," I am in tears. This "God Talk" would change my life. This was all He said, and this was all He needed to say. I didn't grasp the significance of this "God Talk" at the time, but it acted as the catalyst inside of me to revive me from the rut I was in. Now that I am writing about this "God Talk," I know God was not asking me to go on, but He was *telling* me to go on. Instead of being reactive to my life's circumstances, I became proactive. The pain didn't leave me; I left the pain. The will to live was birthed in me by that "God Talk" that day in the schoolyard. I later learned when I was in my twenties that there is a scripture that states, "When my father and my mother forsake me, then the LORD will take me up (Psalm 27:10)."

My cousin, Brenda, is my big sister because that is the way Momma raised us, as a family; we were not cousins but sisters. She worked diligently with me that summer to help me pass my classes. She would drill me on spelling words and she would practice doing math problems with me. I always admired her. She was a true jewel. I got promoted to the fourth grade, but not without some lingering cloud of my erratic behaviors following me. The school must have determined that I still had some serious problems. They removed me from regular classes and placed me in Title One classes.

The power of the "God Talk" in the schoolyard had taken residence deep within me and it was continuously unfolding in me every day. I began to excel in my classes. The school began to question its judgment. I wasn't slow: I was hurt. My mom had left with not so much as a word. On top of all of that, she didn't call or anything. If I did by some chance get a number to call her, she would pretend it wasn't her. At the time, I didn't know where my daddy was. I knew one thing: God was right, and I had to GO ON. I thank God for caring. Thank God for the "God Talk."

I continued to excel in the Title One classes. My teachers soon realized I wasn't slow after all. I was placed back in regular classes by the fifth grade. I continued to excel and I joined a lot of extra-curricular activities. I became a bookworm. I would read the dictionary and the Bible all the time. I was striving to be all I could be. I will never forget the words of my band director, from whom I learned a valuable life insight. He would encourage the class by saying, "While you all are watching TV, remember the people on TV got theirs; you need to be getting yours." I took this statement to heart.

I never was too much of a TV fan; I became a book fan. Just give me a book. I truly believed, as the poet Emily Dickenson said, "There is no frigate like a book." I began to transcend my realities of a small town and escape beyond the horizon of just existing. I was alive and forevermore. Yes, by the ninth grade I was a straight "A" student. The lowest grade I had on my report card was a ninety-eight. My classmates knew me as being smart. I was not only smart, but I started drawing and painting in the third grade and I started writing poems in the seventh grade. I won numerous awards while in school. I graduated with honors and went on to college. Thanks to Mrs. Leonard, my high school counselor, who fostered the idea in me to go further. She died during my first year of college. I graduated from Georgia Southern with honors. Thank God for the "God Talk" on the Waynesboro Elementary schoolyard.

Chapter Three

Progressive Traveling

"God Talks"

"By faith Abraham, when he was called to go out into a place when he should afterwards receive an inheritance, obeyed; and he went out, not knowing whither he went."
~ Hebrews 11:8

I Have Not Gone Anywhere: You Left

I was accepted into Georgia Southern College and was scheduled to start in August of 1988. It was truly a milestone in my life, given all the turmoil that I had endured. This was something off the radar, yet the providential hand of God would propel me on in my destiny. Through the involvement of a very compassionate, caring student counselor, Mrs. Leonard, who was a constant source of encouragement for me, I was enrolled in college. Mrs. Leonard would meet with me and ensure I had the necessary provision to move forward into a higher learning institution. God placed such phenomenal people in my path as signposts to point the way. I can still see her, coming to my classroom, urging all the students to "read, read, and read." Yes, she was famous for those words to a group of rural high school students. I internalized every "read" she ever spoke. She scheduled me for the SAT and procured a voucher to pay for me to take the test. She assisted me with selecting a college and filling out my application for Georgia Southern College. She filled out my financial aid and scholarship materials. Now that I reflect back, she was an instrument of the Lord whom He had given a vision for me that exceeded what I could even see for myself: I was part of her mission. Amazingly, this dear, sweet woman of God went to be with the Lord my first year of college. She would only know through heaven the great impact she had in my life and the far-reaching effect of her ministry to me.

Oh wow, a whole new world: I never knew so much freedom! My grandmother, Eliza always set such boundaries for me: She was strict. There was so much I had yet to experience and so much I was not prepared for. One true foundation I did have was my love for the Lord. God and I were best friends. I had heard and read all about the world in scripture and now I was in the world in a way I had never experienced – without Momma's boundaries. Everything was wide open: I could do anything I wanted, or at least it seemed to be that way. I met so many new people in my dormitory. I connected with so many friends. I started hanging out, listening to worldly music, and going to the campus parties, hanging out late, and clubbing, and I even tried cursing. I had one racy friend from Savannah, who cursed every time she opened her mouth. I was growing up, but to what I didn't know. I even had a boyfriend and I had liberty to be with him, especially since I was at college. I was no longer with Momma.

Momma had run him away when he tried to come to our house to see me. In fact, she scared him away. He told me how one day he came by to see me. Momma was sitting on the porch with her dark shades on, and he approached her and asked if I was home. She told him emphatically, "Don't no Sabrina live here and don't you come back here." Do you know what? He never did. That was Momma, so protective and strict. Now that I look back, I appreciate her boundaries: God used them to shield me for a season.

In my Bible that I inherited from my Aunt Essie in 1981, I wrote a special note to God about our relationship and where I desired to be with Him. I don't recall the exact content of the note, but it was a covenant between the two of us. I took this Bible to college with me. I was spreading my wings in this season. I was learning life and I was in for some valuable lessons in life. There was another godsend in my life and I could never mention these turbulent years without acknowledging the continued impact she had in my life: my Aunt Kin, who has now gone on to be with the Lord. My Aunt Kin was also a mother figure in my life. She worked alongside with Momma, helping to raise everybody. She was as strict as Momma, but I could relate to her better concerning issues I was facing as a young woman. She always advised me and kept me on the straight and narrow as much as she could. She would pull my skirt tail when she saw me venturing too far and getting in danger zones. I don't think we really see the totality of someone's impact in our lives until they are no longer with us. This was so true of my Auntie. As I am writing and reflecting, there are so many pivotal moments of introspection like viewed on a movie screen, and I see "God Talks" through people He divinely places in our lives. My Aunt Kin and her husband, Uncle Tommie, were such people

My first roommate was eccentric. She appeared to be all right at first, but her involvement in a relationship with a nursing student would soon reveal some deeper rooted issues that were quite scary for an unsuspecting roommate such as me, who had never witnessed someone who was suicidal. That's what I will call it. She went off on the deep end when the young man and she broke up. I was not in any position to deal with such things. At the time, I was into Madonna being a "Material Girl" and Prince being an "International Lover," far from the innocent Christian girl who came to college. I had drifted far in my relationship with the Lord and would drift even further before this "God Talk" finished.

My roommate was troubled: She acted as if she had two personalities. I noticed the more she got involved with this young man, the darker her persona became — she appeared obsessive. I don't recall all the details but she had a crisis one night, a total breakdown, and was threatening to commit suicide because of the breakup with the young man. She was in a state of rage and other voices seemed to be speaking through her. It was quite a night as many of us tried to convince her not to take her life. I don't recall what happened, but she moved out of our room. I just didn't feel comfortable. I think she went home and got some help, and I don't recall really seeing her around any more after this incident.

I progressively got deeper into wrong things. Open the door for Satan and he will take over. Things were getting rather chaotic in my life. I moved to another room and one of my home girls, Nancy, became my roommate. I surrounded my side of the room with posters of Prince. "Purple Rain" was what was happening. I learned all the lyrics and would literally perform them. The sexually explicit overtones were consuming me. By this time I was chanting with the chorus, "I would die for you." Prince had proclaimed, "I am your Messiah and that's the reason why, I would die for you."

It was this part of the song that aroused my suspicion that something was amiss. I only knew Jesus as the Messiah and I was confused as to why Prince would use the word "Messiah" to describe himself. I woke up with Prince and went to bed with Prince. I played "Purple Rain" over and over and over again. I was so intrigued with Prince that I did a term paper on Prince to prove that he was not as bad as some religious zealots were making him out to be. I even called my daddy and discussed how religious fanatics were coming to our dormitories, calling Prince a devil. I defended my idol, even though I shared with my daddy that I was confused.

My daddy told me, "God is not the author of confusion." This would prove eye-opening for me. As I worked on my term paper, I read numerous reports of how an audience of over a 100,000 people was singing and motioning, "I would die for you." The reporter described the people to be in a trance-like state and he wondered: would they die for Prince? He went on to discuss the subliminal messages that were translated in songs and mentioned my favorite album at the time, "Purple Rain." He gave instructions on how to listen

45

to the album backwards and hear encoded messages. So, I went to my dorm room and did just that. I put the album on, put the record player on neutral and used my hand to spin the album backwards. I was horrified to hear thunders, cracking sounds of lightning, and sounds of wind roaring, while a creepy voice could be heard saying, "He's Coming," over and over, squeaky and piercing, "He's Coming." The sound was so frightening that I snatched the album off the player.

The realization of what I had gotten myself into over-whelmed me and I ripped every poster from my wall in sheer terror. I sobbed, "Oh Lord, what have I done?" The demon of fear gripped me and snarled at me as if to say, "I am going to get you now that you see — I am not letting you get away." I had a "God Talk" all night — lying almost motionless for fear of being consumed by the darkness that had been exposed in my life. I continued to have "God Talks." I asked God, why was I so far from Him?

Then "God Talked" and said, "Sabrina, I have not gone anywhere, I have been here all along, but you left." "I cried unto the LORD with my voice and He heard me out of His holy hills. Selah. I laid me down and slept; I awakened; For the LORD sustained me (Psalm 3:4-5)." I repented and I was restored. God and I were back together. Just as I was in this moment — God had me pick up my Bible that I had inher-ited from Aunt Essie, with a special note I had written Him years earlier, and there it was: a "God Talk" fulfilled. What I had written to God in 1981 had come to pass in 1987: I had come into a new revelation of God that would take me to a transforming encounter that would leave me forever changed. "Who redeemeth my life from destruction; who crowneth with loving-kindness and tender mercies; Who satisfieth thy mouth with good things; so that thy youth is renewed like the eagles (Psalm 103:4-5)."

Remove Him From My System

I went home for the weekend as usual. God was continuously uncloaking the darkness that had been hidden in my life to bring me back to Him. My boyfriend came over to visit when I arrived home, but rumors had surfaced that while I was away at college, he was dating another young lady and she was pregnant. Word was that her dad was insisting that he marry her or else, so they were married while I was off at school. However, he still had the audacity to show up at my house when I arrived home. At this time, I lived with my sisters, Brenda and Karen, on 8th Street in Waynesboro, Ga. He came to break the news to me that had already been broken. I was so hurt by the betrayal that I remember taking a big silver spoon and hitting him with it. He took the licks graciously and he continued trying to explain to me that I was and always would be his sweetheart — Romeo and Juliet.

Well, we all know how that ended! I had a "God Talk," and as always, "God Talked." I asked God to remove him from my system and yes, He did just as I requested. God took the hurt and the feelings of betrayal. There was no residue left. I felt totally, mysteriously healed! I always knew that if you asked Him in faith, not wavering, He would do it. There would be more hurdles, but I knew with God's help I would press deeper into the things of God.

Look at Your Hands

The enemy saw me getting closer to the Lord, and as always he would work through the things that are in us to exploit our weakness. A young man started looking at me when I would come home. He had a nice new Mustang. He started talking to me. Sometimes as I walked to work, he would pull over and whisper sweet nothings. I saw it all as an attempt to lure me into his den. I wasn't in any committed relationship at the time — just flings, as most people casually would say, "just friends." Yeah, "just friends with fringe benefits," right?

You know the friends who are a little more than friends – just not committed. Oh God, how we deceive ourselves and others. God is faithful: He who began a good work in you is faithful to complete it. It is a process: sanctification is a lifelong process. We never arrive: We are ever arriving at new places in Christ.

I learned that the young man was married, but at the time was separated and going through a divorce. There was this other young man who was married, and he was trying to befriend me also. There were even more suitors, but none of them were good for me and the enemy was using all the attention to entrap me. Since my struggle with obesity was a thing of the past and my newfound frame seemed to put me in a whole new class of popularity, I literally was swarmed with guys who didn't find me attractive at 192 pounds, but were now drooling over me at 132 pounds. One in particular rejected me when I was obese, but I had become a "must have" for him. Honestly, I had a crush on him as a young girl, so it appeared that now I could have him, so why should it be forbidden?

I had always heard people say God saves us just in time.

I had returned to school for the week. I was sitting in my dormitory room at my desk, looking in my mirror, when "God Talked." "Look at your hands: You can't move one finger if I do not allow you." His voice was audible! It was the first time in my life that I felt so beautiful, only to hear "God Talk" and say "all is vanity." Momma had always told me people could see their death, and I thought for certain this was it. The words from Tramaine Hawkins' song rang in my ears: "I was so confused, I thought the end was near."

All this happened that Monday when I returned to school. I remember walking around in a daze. Then Tuesday, I got a call to inform me that the young man with the Mustang had been killed in a car accident. I was overcome with emotions: "Surely God is going to take me." Darkness began to swallow me up. I was in unbelief so much that I called my friend at the funeral home to confirm or disprove the report. I know he was in his early twenties, just a few years older than me. Gone so young, and the reality was even as Momma once told me, "There are long and short graves, you know."

At this time, I was living with my sister Brenda and Karen in a small singlewide trailer on Eighth Street when I came home from college on the weekend to work. I arrived home from College that Friday night, the weight of death permeated the atmosphere. Everyone in the house was sick with the flu. I walked into what seemed like a death camp. Overwhelmed with the feelings of death, I ran to the back of the trailer and fell on my face weeping. Darkness was everywhere. Then "God Talked." He told me to call a missionary I had often observed when she came to the nursing home to minister. I was working my way through college as a nurse aid at Brentwood Nursing Home. I looked her number up in the phone book. I still remember her number over twenty-five years later. She was called Mother Betty. The only thing I asked her was if I could go to church with her. She picked me up the same night.

God already knew they were having service that night. Now, I must make this point. I was a member of Watkinsville Baptist Church, my family church. Everybody was buried there. My great grandmother was buried there and my granddaddy McKinley Mathis was listed in the history of the church. However, God led me in this direction that night. When I went with Mother Betty that Friday night, I saw something I had never experienced in any church. People were exuberantly praising and worshipping God. The people were ecstatically caught up with God. I watched in wonder. I said to myself, "Whatever they've got: I want it," and I was passionately moved to pursue it. How can I have this? I went forward that night and they shared Acts 2:38 with me. That night, I was baptized in Jesus' Name.

Then they took me to the tarrying room. I tarried for the infilling of the Holy Ghost. I had never heard of being filled with the Holy Ghost. As I tarried for some hours in praise and thanksgiving to God, the pastor of the church came to the room to help me. I will never forget the words he spoke: "You believe: God help your unbelief." Then he laid his hands on me and I received the Holy Ghost through the laying on of hands. Words came forth out of my mouth, a heavenly language — a new tongue. I wondered in sheer joy at the sound — astonished and amazed as to what had happened to me that night! Awesome God! As Mother Betty drove us home that night, I felt like a new creature. The darkness was banished and I was basking in the marvelous light of God's glory. I could breathe a breath of relief.

I was unencumbered with the cares of this life: A baby that had just emerged from the womb. How wonderful! The next day would prove adventurous for me. I woke up with so much expectation for the new closeness I had with God. I walked down 8th Street, leaping and praising God. I was alive and I was experiencing life in a way I had never before experienced. I was refreshed and I knew I was going to live. Praise God, I didn't have a death sentence but a life sentence. All the time it seemed as if death was working in me, it was life working in me to bring me to life itself. In the midst of all the excitement there was also a startling new reality: I could literally see sin and how it marred my surroundings. The words of "Amazing Grace" resonated with me on a whole new plain, "I once was blind but now I see."

I ended all the ungodly relationships — you know, with the so-called friends with fringe benefits. I wanted nothing to do with anything that I perceived would not be pleasing and honorable to God. I didn't need the fraudulent substitutes:

the lover of my soul – Jesus — had enraptured me and all I cared about was Him. I learned the highest praise for God was Hallelujah! I wanted everyone to know this joy unspeakable and full of glory!

Bethel Christ Temple Apostolic Church was the name of my new church. I loved Watkinsville Baptist Church, but I knew God had called me to another place in this season. My new church taught separation from the world in a way I had never heard. It was like the honeymoon period was over and the bliss began to fade into rules and regulations that I didn't know initially came with the packet. I was so impressionable, and I was willing to submit to whatever I had to do to maintain my newfound experience. We were taught that we couldn't wear make-up, pants, and jewelry. I willingly submitted. I was holy according to my new church family — holiness meant "set apart"— separated from the world. I went back to Georgia Southern College and took all my make-up, jewelry, and pants and any other forbidden things and dumped them down the trash chute. Funny, how many of my classmates asked for my things, seeing that I was going to throw them away. However, I objected to doing any such thing. I told them if they wanted the items, I couldn't give them to them. I was going to throw them away and if they wanted them, they would have to get them after I threw them away. Guess what? They did exactly that. They waited at the end of the trash chute and gathered as much as they wanted. All I knew was that I was free from sin — or at least so I thought.

Well, my professors and friends took note of the new me who went from stylish to drab. Some of my professors were concerned, until they pulled me aside to inquire about the drastic transformation I had made. I found it hard to dress out for my recreation electives that were very physical and almost impossible to do in a dress and a skirt. I assured them that this was the new, saved me. My Aunt Kin expressed her concerns as well, but I thought none of their concern had any validity. After all, "This is the Lord's doing; it is marvelous in our eyes (Psalm 118:23)."

I started evangelizing Georgia Southern. I was sharing my experiences with everyone — students, professors and all who would give an ear. I would bring young ladies home to get saved. So many came and received Jesus and joined me on my pilgrimage to see other young people saved and delivered. I started Bible study groups and prayer groups. The zeal of my newfound love consumed me. I would preach Jesus everywhere: I was very zealous, to say the least. One day I was in the library trying to persuade some students about the gift of tongues. They laughed me to scorn, but I was compelled all the more to share my experience. I rebuked them sharply for what I perceived as their ignorance. "Oh, the gift is real and God is able to give the gift to you all," I proclaimed. Their obstinacy did not deter me. I had a lot to learn. Opposition didn't deter, it only encouraged me. The love of God was all that mattered and I was willing to suffer persecution for the name of Christ. I was compelled to share my testimonies of "God Talks."

Chapter Four

Mapping New Paths

"God Talks"

"And the Word of the Lord came unto him saying, Get thee hence, and turn thee eastward, and hide thyself by the brook Cherith, that is before Jordan. And it shall be, that thou shalt drink of the brook; and I have commanded the ravens to feed thee there. So he went and did according unto the Word of the Lord: for he went and dwelt by the brook Cherith that is before Jordan. And the ravens brought him bread and flesh in the morning, and bread and flesh in the evening, and he drank from the brook. And it came to pass after the brook dried up, because there had been no rain in the land."

~ 1 Kings 17:2-7

Lump Gone in Three Days

There were many "God Talks" embedded in this season. I began to dream more, experience trances, and signs and wonders followed me. "God Talked" – He told me in a dream that I had a lump in my breast. I woke up that next morning and put my hand directly on the lump. I woke up my sister, Brenda and shared what the Lord had said and I put her hand on the lump. Then "God Talked" and told me the lump would be gone in three days. I went back to Georgia Southern College after being home for the weekend. One of my professors whose nickname was Mouse, with whom I had a close relationship, was very concerned for me. She was already concerned about the transformation I had made to my appearance, but she was even more concerned that I would not seek medical attention for the lump in my breast. I shared with her how the Lord spoke to me concerning the lump and told me that it would be gone in three days. She tried her best to persuade me to go to the doctor. I even shared with her how "God Talked" to me in a dream and told me about the lump. She was not convinced at all and repeatedly expressed concern. Just as "God Talked," the lump was gone in three days. There was no trace of the lump. I will never advise anyone to ignore a lump in their breast, I am just speaking of my experience with "God Talk."

Chain Links Restored

I continued to study the Word of God for five hours at a time. I became a student of the Word. I would lock myself up in a study room at school and study for hours at a time, only taking fifteen-minute breaks. I had learned the discipline of studying from a Chinese student named Victoria, whom I had befriended. Her study technique worked for me. I would set aside five to six hours at a time, studying for forty-five minutes and taking fifteen-minute breaks. It worked for me with my class assignments, and now I would employ it to study God's Word. Read, write, and review: another study technique I had learned in college that would prove instrumental. As I studied, it was as if the words would leap off the pages into my spirit. It was as if the Holy Spirit was reading the words to me and I was absorbing it all like a sponge.

I was satiated with the sincere milk of the Word, but gulping down chunks of meat with it. It was all so nourishing to my spirit. "God Talked" and gave me a prophecy through an open vision of what the church would one day look like. He showed me a chain with links that were cracked and broken. He told me how the enemy had used denominationalism to divide the Body of Christ, but that one day the divisions, the cracks would be healed, and the places of brokenness would be repaired. His people will one day be as one. "God Talked" and told me that back in 1987, and I witnessed this prophetic word come to pass as we found ourselves fellowshipping with other Christians from various denominations in the year 2012.

Walls are being replaced with doors of newfound opportunities to come together and fellowship without respect to denominations, ethnicity, cultural or racial barriers. Barriers that once kept God's people from linking together are constantly being eradicated and will continue to be, until God's people come together in the unity of the faith in Christ Jesus.

Greater is He That is In You

I continued to evangelize the campus of Georgia Southern College. Many young ladies were following me home to Waynesboro, Ga., to get baptized and filled with the Holy Ghost. They were as zealous as I was. We were advancing the kingdom of God across our campus: We were sharing our conversion experience with everyone who would listen, and sometimes with those who wouldn't, in hopes of persuading and convincing all about Jesus. Three of my dearest and closet sisters in the Lord were Monica, Marla, and Avis. Avis, I believed to be more zealous than me. We all loved the Lord. It was all about Jesus. Everything God showed me, I shared with them.

One day we were all gathered in one of our friend's dormitory room for prayer, when suddenly a dear sister in our prayer group began to jerk violently. Her eyes rolled up in the back of her head and went completely white. Her head wove back and forth. A man's voice – deep and rustic – spoke through her. This voice began to prophesy to all of us in the room. It told us many great things concerning our future, and admonished us not to tell anyone of this experience. When the voice finished speaking, my dear sister ceased the convulsion-like motions. She appeared oblivious to what had just taken place. She looked spaced out – like in a daze. There was a glazed look still in her eyes. All of us were looking around at each other, bewildered by all that had just transpired.

She left the room while the rest of us stayed back. I counseled everyone concerning what had just happened. "God Talked," and He revealed to me that what we had just witnessed was demonic powers presenting themselves as a messenger from God, and that we were not to receive anything that was said as from God but the devil. Then the Lord led me to go call my pastor and tell him of what had just happened. Everyone followed me to another sister's room. I could not understand how this could be, seeing that this was one of the sisters who had come home with me and had accepted the Lord as her savior and been baptized. However, at that time I was very young in the Lord. After many years of experience in ministry, I have seen many Christians demonized — under the influence of a demon or demons: I now know and understand how this could be. However, I didn't know what I know now in regards to this type of manifestation. After all, I was a babe in Christ and things on this level should not be happening, or so I thought.

The one thing that God pointed out was how this spirit sought to work through secrecy. The spirit said, "Don't tell" anyone, and that was the "giveaway." The enemy was trying to trap us, and God only knows the deception he would have worked had not "God Talked" and exposed him.

"God Talked" and let me know through a Word of Knowledge that my dear friend had left but would return soon, and we had very little time to prepare for her return. It was imperative to consult my pastor because I felt that this manifestation was out of my league. I placed the call to my pastor and told him all about the manifestation. I was expecting that he would make a special trip to Statesboro from Waynesboro, about an hour's drive, but not so. I presumed that something of this magnitude required a more seasoned saint. He simply said to me, "Greater is he that is in you than he that is in the world" (1 John 4:4). I was taken aback by his response at first – like what? Then he repeated it without further instructions and then hung up the phone. I looked around at everyone and "God Talked," giving me specific directions as to what I needed to do. I urged everyone by saying we had to move swiftly, and I began to give everyone their assignment.

We went back to Marla's and my room. No sooner had we settled what each person's assignment was, the knock came at the door. It was our dear sister. She was as puzzled as ever. She recognized that something had happened, but was confused about the entire matter. I reached out to her in love and asked her to sit on the foot of my bed. I let her know we were expecting her, that "God Talked" and told me she would come soon. I explained to her how Jesus loved her and we all did as well. I also explained to her how the manifestation earlier was not of the Lord and something else had taken control of her. Before I could finish speaking, the demon threw her back on the bed and her eyes rolled up in her head until all we could see was the whites of her eyes.

I took authority in the name of the Lord Jesus and commanded the demon to stop, and it obeyed. She sat back up and looked at me. I continued to express the love of God to her as others in the room were praying and some pleading the blood of Jesus. Then the demon interfered again. I commanded the demon this time not to speak again unless I spoke to it, and I continued to minister to my sister. The Lord guided me through the whole session, which I now know to be a deliverance session. I found out from my sister that she had an imaginary friend when she was a young child. She explained to me how she derived companionship from her friend, and she had no idea at the time that it was a demon. That was how he gained entrance in her life. She told me it felt like her throat was a thermometer, with mercury moving back and forth.

During this session, I would talk to my friend and I would also talk to the demon until "God Talked" and led me to end the session. The Lord did not lead me to cast the demon out. I made plans to bring her home with me to my church so that she could be delivered. I had believed that God would have more experienced saints cast the demon out. I sought help for her, but to my dismay no one could deliver her – not even my pastor. When I got back to school, "God Talked" through my sister Avis, saying, "her deliverance is not for everybody else: God wants to use you." It was true, I had taken her everywhere else and it all came directly back to me. "God Talked," releasing the know-how needed for my friend's deliverance. He gave to me further instructions regarding my assignment with my friend. He led me to take her walking and spend time just feeding her the Word. He let me know the Word of God would displace the demon.

I just had to feed her the Word, and the more Word she received into her spirit, the fuller she would become on the Word until the demon would be driven out. This took a couple of weeks, but it worked beautifully. A "God Talk" fulfilled. She became full of God's Word and was liberated. She befriended a true friend, Jesus, through the knowledge of His Word, and the demon lost his status. Who needs an imaginary friend when you can have a real friend? The demon was no friend from the beginning, he just exploited the innocence of a child and took advantage of her in her youth. Thank God for "God Talks."

The Angels on The Ship

There were still so many fears embedded in me from my past. I dared not tell a soul for fear of being laughed at. I was so ashamed. How could a twenty-one-year-old Upward Bound camp counselor break the news to her students that she was afraid to ride the elevator or escalators? Some things I had conquered in my saved life, and yet some things still haunted me, as if they would catch me and swallow me whole.

It was time for the finale of the Upward Bound Camp. The students had chosen to go on a tour of the Carolinas. This was definitely exciting for me, because the furthest I had ever been north of Waynesboro was Augusta. I was overjoyed with the excitement of having the opportunity to travel.

I was always talking to God. At this point, He and I were the best of friends. I talked to Him all the way on the bus trip to Charleston. I sang my songs and admired the scenery on the way. Oh my, how God talks through His creation. It was history in the making, and yet Charleston offered so much history to see. I was like a child in a candy stored, "oohing" and wowed by everything. I imagined my students were probably like me.

It wasn't until we checked in at the hotel that I was confronted with my fear of the elevator. To get to my room, I had to take an elevator. I quickly figured out an alternative: Stairs. "Thank You, Jesus," I was spared the embarrassment. So guess what? I took the stairs. I had a way of minimizing without someone noticing what I was doing. I would kind of sneak off, and before they would notice, I was from one floor to the other floor, as I needed to be. I was so scared!!!

Then as if the terror wouldn't end, the highlight of our trip was taking a tour on a ship out into the ocean. How I would deal with this remained to be seen. There were no stairs to escape to. The thought of even boarding a boat was like certain death to me. I was having a "God Talk" the entire time, but for a moment even that wasn't easing the terror. I wasn't going to be able to hide this one. I was going to have to risk someone knowing about how fearful I was. I confided in Mr. Gunter, the director of the Georgia Southern Upward Bound Program. The tightening of my chest eased up a little, but I could still feel the pressure in my head. I felt faint. "Ooh Lord, don't let me fall out, please don't let me fall out." I sat down next to Mr. Gunter on the back of the ship. I knew God's Word. Whether or not it had sunk in my heart was another matter. I sat trembling, quoting, "Ye are of God little children, and have overcome them because greater is he that is in you than he that is in the world (1 John 4:4)." Something had to happen. I knew "God Talks" always saved me, and I was certain "God Talks" wouldn't fail me now.

I couldn't move. I felt stuck in place. My whole world was standing still. If I could only get some relief, before all of my students discovered the crisis I was in. All of a sudden, I felt this surge in my spirit and I had an unction by God to get up and go to the lower level of the ship. I didn't even question Him. I only prayed now that my limbs would cooperate. The first thing I did was stand up. I felt like Peter walking on the water. I was on my feet, or rather I was on God's feet. I took one step and then another, and finally was walking down to the lower level of the ship. I made it! I saw a lot of my students sitting on one side, but strangely, I was not drawn to sit with them. It was as if my feet were programmed by God to go in the opposite direction, and they brought me to an older couple I didn't even know — "But did I?" I sat by them as if they were old friends. Then the older lady turned to me and said, "Why are you so afraid?" My heart dropped. How did she know? Everything within my soul came out. I began with, "I am so afraid, I am afraid of this ship, the elevators, the escalators – everything."

She looked me in the eyes and she said to me, "You will no longer confess fears from this time on. You are not afraid. You are only afraid because you are telling yourself you are afraid. Say, 'I am not afraid.'" As she talked, it was as if every fear left. I got up without hesitation and began to walk around the ship like a new person. It was liberating indeed: I walked all around the ship. I even went back upstairs on the deck. I had no fear.

The ship came into the harbor. The trip had ended. I was so anxious to get back to the hotel so I could ride the elevator. I had to find the lady God had used to deliver me. She was coming off the ship. I ran to her and grabbed her, exclaiming all the good news of how I didn't feel afraid anymore. I wanted to keep in contact with her always. I couldn't let her get away from me. Strangely, her male companion never said anything. Even when I was getting information from her so I could write to her, he didn't speak. When she finally embraced me, something went all through me. I felt a sense of being loved like I had never experienced in my life. I was overwhelmed by the moment and didn't want her to let me go. I liken that hug to a mother saying a final good-bye to her child who she would never see again. That's how I felt inside — I just didn't want her to ever let go, but she did.

The elevator at the hotel was waiting for me and I was ready. As soon as I got back to the hotel, I stepped onto the elevator with my students. They did not seem to think it was strange because I guess I hid it so well. When we got up to the floor, they stepped off but I stayed on. I was giggling inside. It was a laugh I couldn't keep inside. I burst out in sheer joy, taking no thought about who saw me or heard me. My "God Talk" had paid off and I was free. I rode the elevator up and down — up and down over and over again, as if to let it know I was no longer afraid of it.

Well, the trip was over and we boarded the bus to go back home. I praised God all the way. I just kept singing, "Yes Lord." I cried and thanked God over and over. This was truly a victory for me, and I felt like heaven had broken me out of just one more jail that I was locked in, within my soul. I knew the reasons the elevator had terrorized me so much; it was "the dark room" my mom would lock my siblings and me in all those years. I finally was free from that "dark room" that had dominated so much of my life.

I got home with only one thing on my mind and that was to write the lady who spoke to me on the ship. I had to establish contact with her. I found the paper I had scribbled her address on; it was a South Carolina address. Just as I went to write her, God talked to me. He said, "You can write, but she won't write back because that which you entertained is an angel." Of course, God knew me, I had to write, but I knew that she would not write back. I did and I never got a return or heard from her again. I know God has that letter, and one day He may share it with me.

Chapter Five

Crossing Religious Overpasses

"God Talks"

"Howbeit in vain do they worship me, teaching for
doctrines the commandments of men. For laying
aside the commandments of God, ye hold the
tradition of men, as the washing of pots, and cups:
and many other such like things ye do. And he said
unto them, Full well ye reject the commandment of
God, that ye may keep your own tradition."
~ Mark 7:7-9

Supernatural Hair Growth

I have come to see that anything we put our trust in other than God, He will allow it to be spoiled, whether people, places, or things. Our trust must rest solely in Him. I was growing in the Lord in Bethel Christ Temple. It seemed anything I asked God to do would happen. I didn't recognize it, but I was becoming spiritually spoiled. I had such favor with God and man: I grew and increased in stature day by day. I didn't like my appearance as much. I was adhering to all the rules that my church required, but I couldn't understand why I still desired to wear make-up, pants, and jewelry. Then I began to question whether something was wrong with me for having those desires. My spirit just wouldn't rest. I was always so fashionable. The struggle became more intense. I would suppress these urges as sinful, but "God Talked" and led me to study the scriptures to see where it was sinful to wear these things. I fasted, prayed and studied.

During this season, I was working at school through work study at Georgia Southern at a restaurant called Sarah's, I was working at the nursing home in Waynesboro-Brentwood Terrace, and I was cleaning house for a dear, sweet lady in Waynesboro, Mrs. Mobley. I would come home and work sixteen hours on Saturday, and sometimes eight on Sunday, go to church, return to school late Sunday night, and report to work by 6:00am that morning. Somehow in the midst of all that, I managed to clean the houses of Mrs. Mobley and sometimes her friend, Mr. Neely. During all this time, I managed a full class load of sixteen to eighteen credit hours per quarter. The Lord also blessed me to make the Dean's List most of the time. I graduated with a 3.2, even though I worked so hard: It was Jesus! Before I started working, I didn't have money for food or my necessities. My Aunt Kin would often send me $15 a week until I started working. God always provided for me. There was always a ram in the bush.

That ram for me in that season was the Pattersons and a precious lady named Ida Sello — a God-sent "God Talk." Many days I would be sitting in the library and she would walk up, hug me, and sit down at the table with me to chat for a minute. She always called me Mrs. Georgia Southern. She had worked in the Burke County School System. I think she was taking graduate courses. She was always so kind and compassionate toward me. She saw my struggles and gave of herself to help me. She would always slip me money under the table and smile — sometimes $20, and sometimes a little more. That was a lot to a struggling student. That would buy me a meal or two.

All my sisters came home and it was like a family reunion. We were all gathered over at Momma's house. It was almost surreal not seeing Momma in the blockhouse. She had finally left 106 10th Street. Momma was in an apartment and she seemed to have adjusted. We took a lot of family pictures. My hair was broken off so badly. This only added to my appearance dilemma. I stood out like a sore thumb and everyone noticed the change in my appearance, but not near as much as I did.

I was at work at the nursing home and "God Talked." I went into the restroom behind the front nursing station and I had a "God Talk." I knelt down and I said, "Lord, You know every strand of hair on my head; you have them all numbered and I know you have the power to make them grow." Then

"God Talked" and told me to sow the hair that was on my head for new hair. "God is not mocked: for whatsoever a man sows: that shall he also reap" (Galatians 6:7). He wanted me to rely on sowing and reaping with my hair. So, I did just that.

My sisters and I went to Thelma Howard and she cut off all my hair to only one inch long, in tiny little layers that she slightly bent to the side. My head looked gigantic with no hair, but I trusted God: I didn't even question Him. I had peace about obeying God in this matter. Peace always accompanies obedience.

My sisters and I were sitting in Long John Silvers in Augusta. We were laughing and having fun, when suddenly I had a Word of Knowledge about my hair that I blurted out. I said to them, "My hair will be down my back by Christmas." It was at the beginning of September when I made the statement. I didn't take my senior pictures because I didn't like how short my hair was. Suddenly, my hair started to grow rapidly. There were times that it felt like someone was pulling my hair out of my head. I could literally feel my hair growing – like it was crawling out of my hair follicles, a weird sensation that I constantly felt. No one believed it was my hair. Many times at work at Sarah's, people would comment about how fast my hair was growing and suspected I added a weave, but I would quickly hold my head over for them to witness the miracle. One day at a family gathering, my granddaddy questioned whether or not my hair was real. So, I politely flipped my head over for him to examine. Everywhere I went, people took notice of my hair. Finally, Christmas came and my hair was down my back. "God Talked" and gave a sure Word that proved to be sure in the end.

Pay That Which You Vow

That was just part of the transformation. Now back to the struggle over the pants, make-up, and jewelry. My faith was all the more emboldened through this "God Talk" One day, I was cleaning Mrs. Mobley's house. I was praising and exalting God when I was caught up speaking in diverse tongues. At that moment, "God Talked" and said, "When you vow a vow unto God, defer not to pay it, for he has no pleasure in fools: Pay that which you have vowed. Better it is that you should not vow, than that you should vow and not pay. Permit not your mouth to cause your flesh to sin, neither say before the angels that it was an error: Why should God be angry at your voice, and destroy the works of your hand? (Ecclesiastes 5:4-6)" "God Talked" and told me to take this message to my pastor.

Up until this point, I readily obeyed God, but this time I was like, "little ole me? I am just a babe," and "I can't go to my pastor and tell him that." So I didn't go. Well, God doesn't change His mind. He meant for me to go, and since I didn't go, He orchestrated circumstances in such a manner that would bring them to me.

I had started wearing little earrings despite the customs at my church. Through my exhausted studies, I had learned that Paul said, "If any man seem to be contentious, we have no such custom, neither does the churches of God" (1 Corinthians 5:16). I had come to see all the rigidness as customs imposed on the people — legalism. I had come to understand that jewelry, make-up, and pants did not have power to condemn people to hell and was not a plan of salvation. The truth had enlightened my darkness. I was walking in liberty that is in Christ Jesus. My wearing the little earrings enraged some. I was only seeking to do as Paul preached — moderation.

It was time for the Exchange Club Fair in Burke County. Excitement always filled the air around fair time. There wasn't much to do in Burke County so the Burke County Exchange Club Fair was a huge deal, and it had always been that way as far as I could remember from a child. My sisters and I had made preparations to take the children to the fair. When I woke up that morning, the Holy Spirit strongly impressed upon me to go on a fast. Then "God Talked" and gave me a Word of Knowledge that I would have some visitors that day. He even told me that one of those visitors would be my pastor. I shared this with my sisters: I told them that I would have some visitors come by. They had grown quite accustomed to how God operated in my life, so they knew something was up. Sure enough, I was fasting when some time that afternoon, my sister, Brenda informed me that someone was outside to see me.

I went outside and immediately recognized it was my pastor's van. "God Talked," and told me to go with them. As I approached the van, I recognized there were two other men, ministers with my pastor from our church. They opened the door and greeted me, but would not get out of the van. Instead, they asked me if I could come and go with them. I was a little hesitant at first, seeing that it was three men ministers, but "God Talked" and gave me leave to go with them, assuring me that He was present with me. I entered the van, but I didn't remove my earrings. They all greeted me: "Praise the Lord."

As soon as we pulled away from my house, my pastor proceeded to tell me the purpose of the meeting. He stated that the reason for them meeting with me was to discuss my wearing earrings to church and that some of the saints were really disturbed by my doing so. I knew very different. God had set this meeting up so that I would deliver the message He had for me to deliver. I learned that sometimes when God tells you to do something and you don't do it, He will bring it to you.

I understood what God required of me and that He was providing the platform for the message. I looked at my pastor in his eyes and I told him that, "You're not here about my earrings." Indeed it might have been the matter that he believed he had come for, however, God had shown me otherwise. I told him of the day that I cleaned Mrs. Mobley's house and how the Lord had caught me up and I was speaking in diverse tongues and God gave me a word to give him the scripture, Ecclesiastes 5:4-6, and that God said, "Pay that which thou hast vowed."

He looked at me as if to mock me. I maintained the Word that the Lord had sent me to give. He stated to me, "You are just a babe in the Lord." I continued to tell him of the wisdom God gave Solomon above many that were his seniors. His countenance changed as if he pondered what he had walked into. So he began to explain to me how God was leading him to divorce his wife and marry another evangelist in our church. Then the whole matter was exposed as to why God gave me such a Word to give him. Again, I told him "God said, neither say thou before the angels that it was an error." He grew even more agitated with me and told me that this was not about him, it was about me wearing jewelry. I further explained to him that the church operated like a cult, with isolation and legalism, and that Paul taught that the churches of God had no such customs. Then they admitted that there were no scriptures that prohibited one from wearing these things, that they were only customs. Exactly! I expressed to them if my earrings took the saints' minds off of God, then perhaps their minds really weren't on God, and if that were the case, my earrings were very powerful! They were glad to get me back home. They put me out and went on their way.

More and more, the news of his adulterous affair went throughout Waynesboro. Perhaps that day God had me give him that message, God was giving him time to repent. Instead, he went forward with his plans. I remembered God did not allow me to go back to the church the Wednesday night he was making the announcement about his intent. It was a dark season for the people of God. The saints were scattered. I recalled the warning to the pastors who scattered God's sheep. Many were like sheep having no shepherd. I was one: I had nowhere to turn. People were really hurting. Some stayed and some left, but God had promised me that He would shut that place down, and so He did. It wasn't long before padlocks were on the church. It was said that he left town.

All the turmoil led to a season of disillusion for me. It would take the prayers of many intercessors in secret to sustain me during this time. One night, I was at El Bethel Apostolic Church under the leadership of Elder Lloyd. An apostle had come to address the church since many people fled to El Bethel for refuge. In fact, I didn't know it, but Bethel Christ Temple was a church split from saints who had left El Bethel. Now so many of them were back and needed refuge. The apostle urged the saints that they needed to be under a pastor. I realize "God Talked" through the apostle that night, and I joined El Bethel Apostolic Church.

Chapter Six

Up and Downhill

"God Talks"

"And I will strengthen them in the LORD: And they shall
walk up and down in His Name saith the LORD."
~ Zechariah 10:12

"And there came a man of God, and spake unto the King of
Israel, and said, Thus saith the LORD, Because the Syrians
have said, The LORD is God of the hills, but not of the val-
leys, therefore will I deliver all this great multitude into
thine hand, and ye shall know that I am the LORD."
~ 1 Kings 20:28

Ask Me For a House

I was a single mom. My son, Rardietrick was two years old. I had exhausted what little funds I had going back and forth to see my mom, who was terminally ill with cancer at the time. She had since then passed away. I had desired a new house for my son and me, but that would have to be put on hold, or so I thought.

Prior to hearing about my mom's illness, my friends, Teresa, Jeff, and I had been looking at mobile homes. I recall one home in particular that we flipped over. It was gorgeous. I also remember the uniqueness of the house. It had cabinets that hung from the ceiling over the long island that seemed to almost span the entire length of the kitchen. It also had a fireplace with a built-in entertainment cabinet and a bookcase that went from wall to wall. All the wood was cherry in color. The rooms were huge compared to my singlewide. We were sold on it until the salesperson said what it cost, and then we were out of there. After many months of looking, we abandoned the quest. The mobile homes I wanted I couldn't afford, and the ones I could afford I didn't want.

I wanted badly to get out of my singlewide that was at the time falling apart. I actually was afraid for my son, because ants and wasps were all but taking over. My son's crib was in my bedroom next to my bed. One day, wasps were flying all around the room. Thank God he wasn't in his crib at the time, but he very well could have been. I had to close my bedroom door to keep them from taking over the entire house. I called my friend, Elder Williams. He came and discovered that the wasps had infested the insulation in the walls and were getting in my bedroom through a hole in the wall panel. I was frustrated, trapped. My spirit cried out to God, but with my mouth I never uttered a word. It was an unspoken statement. "Lord, I don't want to be here another year." I know God hears us even when we don't speak a word...

One Tuesday almost a year later, on my way from work while traveling on Highway 25, God started a "God Talk." He spoke audibly, as He had sometimes in the past when we had "God Talks." He just started conversing with me. He said, "Sabrina asks me for a house." Now that I am writing about this "God Talk," I am almost baffled how revelations and insights unfold. He didn't say, "The house you saw almost a year ago," but "A house." I responded, "Lord, I don't ask You for material things." He said, "Why, don't you believe I will do it?" Then He said, "Ask me." I said, "Okay, I will ask You."

Providentially, the day of this "God Talk" was Tuesday and El Bethel Apostolic Church's prayer night. Notice I said, "Providentially," not "Coincidentally," because I know nothing happens by coincidence, but God orders the affairs of men after the counsel of His own will. He had orchestrated a plan that was now being implemented by Him and Him alone. I couldn't wait to get to church that night. Prayer service was seven o'clock that evening. I was anxiously awaiting my next "God Talk." I took my son to my Aunt Kin's house as always, so she could babysit him. I headed to prayer service filled with expectancy. Yes, when "God Talks," you should expect God to show up and show out.

I knelt down as always in my spot. Laugh. Everybody knows we claim spots in church. My "God Talk" was really brief that night. I said, "God, You told me to ask You for a house, so I am asking You for a house." The next thing I heard

God say was, "Get up and go get your house." I took Him literally and got up from my "God Talk" to go get my house. I sat praising Him in my corner while others continued with their "God Talk." For me, church was over that night and I was waiting for the next day to go get my house.

The next morning, I was up early. I didn't have any money and I didn't have a deed to some land. What I did have was a "God Talk." A word from the Lord and that, my friends, was more than enough. I was ecstatic. Let me not be cute about it, I was foolish. I went by my job at Gracewood. At the time my boss was Ms. Bogan, and she was one of the best. I love her and respect her highly. I went to her office and exclaimed, "I can't work today, I have to go get my house." She looked at me under her glasses as if she knew there was no stopping me, because she often had witnessed how I was when it came to God. She didn't question me but granted me leave for the day.

When I left her office, I had no idea of where I was going, but I knew God would order my steps. "The steps of a good man are ordered by the Lord: and he delighted in his way (Psalm 37:23)." Just almost a year ago, I had gone to Thompson, Georgia; Aiken, South Carolina, and Augusta, Georgia. This time, the Spirit of the Lord had impressed upon me to go to Gordon Highway to Environs, located in Augusta. So, that was where I went. When I arrived there, the gate was locked. All of a sudden, a man came to the gate as if he was waiting for me.

I said to him, "I want a house with a den in it. I don't have any money and I don't have a deed to any land. All I have is a deed to a twelve by sixty single wide."

He opened the gate and introduced himself as J.T. He walked me down a row with houses on both sides. We passed by about six to seven houses on my left and right, when he finally made a left and there we were in front of a huge double wide home. He opened the door and we walked in the living room. It was impressive. I liked it. Then we walked in the kitchen and family room area. When we did, I was awestruck.

There were those cabinets hanging from the ceiling over the long island bar that stretched almost the length of the whole kitchen. I turned and saw the fireplace, and by this time I was trembling. Oh my "God Talk," everything came back to me in a moment. This was the same house Teresa, Jeff, and I had looked at almost a year ago. I was dismayed. J.T. was still talking. However, at that point I was caught up. He continued the tour and walked me into the master bedroom and bath. The room was big and the garden tub was breathtaking. I could remember him quoting the price of that house when Teresa, Jeff, and I looked at it at $75,000. I could also remember how we made haste to leave.

This time as we walked back into the kitchen, he said to me, "How does fifty-nine-nine sound?" I couldn't speak as he continued talking, telling me that they would even include the furniture package and the appliances with a washer and dryer. I was overcome and still couldn't speak. He completed the tour of the other end of the house and gave me a sold sign and said to place it in the window in what would become my guest bedroom. He had not even taken so much as my name down — no credit application — nothing. All he knew at that moment was Miss. Lewis.

We walked back to the office and he took information to file my application with the bank. Funny, I wasn't afraid, but I knew my credit had some blemishes. We filled out the application around one p.m. I left Environs without a care in the world. The next day, J.T. called to inform me that my loan was approved at six o'clock the same day. He said, "The house is yours."

I was reveling in excitement and praises to God. I couldn't stop thanking Jesus! Just like that, it was mine and we established a delivery date. My "God Talk" had brought me from a twelve by sixty to a twenty-eight by seventy; 1,977 square feet of living space. It was beautiful. It was God's gift to a struggling single mom.

God had a plan for this house. Over the years, it would become the host place for many "God Talks." I remember how the enemy tried to rob me of it several times. One time it was through a young man who proposed to me, who insisted that I sell my house to my daddy and move into his mobile home. I wasn't convinced that this was a part of God's plan for me, so I told him I needed time. One day during a "God Talk," God gave me the answer. I was in my living room and God said, "Look around you; all this I have given you." Then He led me to go outside to my rose flower bed and I heard him say, "Look up, look from one end to the other. See, all this I have given to you and no man can take it from you." God knew I felt like this man was trying to take something from me that I knew He gave to me, and I had never said that to anyone. It was like this man was competing with me. The answer to the proposal was emphatically no.

God already knew that it would not be long after this, within the space of two years, that He would ask me, "What is in your hands?" He knew that this same house would become the Heart of Jesus Church for a season, long before I had any indications. He also knew I would go through many more devastating seasons in my life that would ultimately bring me to that season, but as always, "God Talks" would provide guidance for me on the journey.

God has a sense of humor. After living in the house several years I had a "God Talk" that surprised me. He gave me more insight about the "God Talk" that led me to asking for my house. He said, "You could have had any house, even a $300,000 house because I had to honor my Word. That is where your sight was. Next time, set your sight higher." I could have gone through ten floors! I was like the person in the movie who was given three wishes and uses all three before wishing for more wishes. All I could say was, "God, can we do this again?"

Oh, for those of you who might want to know, Teresa and Jeff got their house within weeks of me getting my house.

Chapter Seven

U-Turns Allowed

"God Talks"

"And he came to himself, and he said, How many
hired servants of my father's have bread enough
and to spare and I perish with hunger! I will arise
and go to my father, and will say unto him, Father,
I have sinned against heaven and before thee, And
am no more worthy to be called thy son: Make me
as one of thy hired servants. And he arose and came
to his father. But when he was yet a great way off,
his father saw him, and had compassion, and ran,
and fell on his neck, and kissed him."
~ Luke 15: 17-20

The Three Deer

I had developed an attitude with God. Things were just not happening for me as fast as I thought they should. I had grown weary in waiting. Day by day, things just seemed to stay the same. It looked like God had taken a vacation on me. I heard a message by T.D. Jakes during this season that resonated with me more than anything. His messages seemed to define this season for me. He described such a season as a "Dry Season."

A preacher can't control what one gleans from his message. When our vision is cloudy, everything is blurred and we can walk away with some warped impressions. That was exactly what I did. I walked away with some warped impressions. I concluded I was indeed in a dry season and nothing was happening in my life. God was quiet. He wasn't saying anything or doing anything, or at least that was what I perceived. I was moping! I was a spiritually spoiled child. God had always moved expeditiously on my behalf. I now know, He was just revealing more of Himself — His character. Imagine if I knew then what I know now. I guess the irony of it all is I wouldn't know what I know about God now without all these teachable moments. Needless to say, I was in for a roller coaster ride.

I went to church that Sunday with a serious attitude. Normally, I always would sit on the front row at church and be jubilant, but this Sunday I purposed to sit in the back near the door — major attitude. I had already said in my mind that I wasn't going up for prayer. God knows our thoughts afar off. You can't fool God! Elder Danner was our interim pastor. He had been appointed to our church. I needed deliverance and I thank God for Elder Danner. When he concluded his message that Sunday, he deviated from the normal course of things, and instead of asking who wanted prayer, the Spirit led him to call for everyone in the church to come to the altar. I was busted! I couldn't possibly just sit back there and not go up, or I would be found out. In a way, I wanted to be found out. I wanted to be exposed so perhaps I could be helped. I reluctantly went up to the altar.

The Spirit of the Lord used Elder Danner awesomely. He anointed everyone with oil and one by one he prayed for us. When he came to me, I remember he paused for a moment and then "God Talked" through this man of God. He said, "All God has done for you, you still don't believe Him. Despite all the Word that is in you, you still question Him. This day you will see. Before the day is over, you will know."

I cried. However, the real issue was trust. After all I had witnessed that God has done in my life, I still had a trust issue. What more could God do?

I left church somewhat despondent. Yes, God knew how I felt, but what would He do about it, seeing I didn't trust him? Is it an all or nothing? I often found in my friendship with God that there were some things I readily believed Him for, and then there were things I struggled with. How I longed to get to a place where I never stumbled in my faith and believed God always in all things. I longed deeply for such a place. Was it even possible to never falter in faith?

In the process of writing my "God Talks," I read a book, ***Hind's Feet in High Places,*** by Hannah Hurnard. I discovered I was so much like "Much-Afraid." I now know it is a process from faith-to-faith, and God is much obliged to see us through until we develop "Hind's Feet." I also know now that there is such a place of trust.

My son Dee and I went home after church as usual. At the time I drove a white Mazda 626, and it was a sight to behold. My son was five years old at that time, and he often described my car as the car with the dents on it — a dent here and a dent there. Needless to say, it served the purpose: it got us from point A to B. During this time, I was hustling. If I could make it, I could sell it. I had a knack for selling things from childhood. I was labeled the "Wheeler Dealer" in high school. I had to do what I had to do to take care of my son, and God always blessed me with talents so that I never had to resort to using others to do it. I was always grateful for that. I was a hard worker. I had a floral order to deliver that Sunday to one of my customers. So after Dee and I rested, I took him and our little cousin Diquan, who was the same age as Dee, and loaded the car up to make the delivery.

It was about 6:30 that evening. We started up Highway 25. Highway 25 was such a strategic place for so many of my "God Talks." I had traveled no more than three miles up the highway, when suddenly three deer were crossing my path. I was traveling sixty-five miles per hour and things happened so fast that there was no way I could stop. For a split second, I braced myself for what seemed like an eternity. There was a loud "Boom!" Three deer were splattered everywhere. The sound of crushing metal and screams filled me with horror at what was flashing right before my eyes. Then a silence, followed by the realization that I was still clutching the steering wheel and my son and my little cousin were all right.

The silence didn't last. Just as fast as it came, it vanished, and "God Talked." "Don't you ever say I am not at work: Even when it looks like I am not at work, I am always at work." I was drenched with tears for relief that "God Talked" and that He had kept my son, my cousin and me from harm, but more than anything, "God Talked." What a relief, "God

Talked." The providential care of God had preserved us. I realized had I swerved in either direction, we would have with all probability been killed. There were oncoming cars on the two-lane highway meeting us in the opposite lane and there was a steep embankment.

Complete strangers were rushing to our aid and someone called the Sheriff's Department. The deer blood and pulp were everywhere. My car and the highway were plastered. The smell from it all was nauseating, and although I was glad that we were alive, I hurt so much for the poor deer. Two mangled bodies lay in the highway and one deer had leaped away, disappearing into the woods during the crash. The officer came and did an accident report. I was visibly shaken and still clinging to Dee and Diquan. My front end was smashed in and the car was covered. It was a mess. To my dismay, I got back in the car and it actually cranked up. It didn't look drivable, but I drove it home.

I called my Uncle Tommie and Aunt Kin and told them about what happened. He asked me could I drive it to town and, unbelievably, I did. He took one look at it and told me that the insurance adjuster would more than likely total the car. That was not what I wanted to hear, since I was almost finished paying for it, but I had learned a powerful lesson that day and that was that God is always at work. I wasn't troubled, but rather trusting and believing that He would work it out for the good.

God brought back to my remembrance how I was dissatisfied about my Mazda 626 car. It was shameful how it was all banged up. I had an unspoken request in my heart and dared to ask God about it because I knew I couldn't afford it. God had often answered unspoken requests for me. There were times He would unction me to ask, and then there were times He just answered my heart without me ever saying a word. This was one of those times. I had no idea how I was to travel to our upcoming family reunion. God blessed me with my next car — a Nissan Altima. I was blown away! Now my son wouldn't have to describe my car as the one with the big dent and the little dent. It was just in time for our annual family reunion, which was scheduled to take place in Miami, Florida.

"God Talked" through situations and circumstances and He always has more in store for us than we dare think or ask.

Chapter Eight

Swerves and Curves

"God Talks"

"And she said unto them, Call me not Naomi, call me
Mara: for the Almighty hath dealt very bitterly with
me. And I went out full, and the Lord hath brought
me home again empty: why then ye call me Naomi,
seeing the Lord hath testified against me, and the
almighty hath afflicted me? So Naomi returned, and
Ruth the Moabitess her daughter in law, with her, which
returned out of the country of Moab: And they came to
Bethlehem in the beginning of the barley harvest."
~ Ruth 1:20-22

When I Get Ready For Something To Happen

God knows what we desire. God also knows what we are not always ready to have. I have learned a lot about God through "God Talks," during times I was insisting on having my way. I did not instantly arrive at the place of trusting God's timing. I wrestled with Him often concerning my desire for a mate. Sometimes I laughed, sometimes I cried, but I learned to wait on the Lord — still waiting!

There are several "God Talks" I have had that reveal a lot about God and His timing. "For my thoughts are not your thoughts, neither are your ways my ways, saith the LORD (Isaiah 55:8)." Just when we think we "got it," He reveals more. It is true, we never arrive, but we are always striving. He is so dimensional: when we stuff Him in one way, He comes out another way. It's useless, people! We might as well admit it. God can't be contained in the things He has made: He contains everything.

I was miserable waiting. I had often watched others and how happy they appeared to be with their mates. Next to desiring my mother, there was nothing else I longed for more than having a husband. I romanticized the whole idea of a mate, and I could not fathom why God was withholding my mate. Oh yes, I knew I had one coming because of "God Talks" over the years. My problem was that I was always trying to force the moment. I was always trying to help God.

I am laughing even as I am writing this, because now I see the folly of it all. However, even in our foolishness, God is God. He is long-suffering and not willing that we should perish, but rather that we should be saved. He bears with us in our unenlightened state. Why wouldn't He be God? After all, He is the one who enlightens us.

I was miserable. Well, let me clarify, I was miserable whenever I thought on why I didn't have a husband. I was in the church van, and we were coming back from visiting a church over in South Carolina. I had taken a tape along so we would have some inspirational music to listen to. I felt like the only single in the van. Many times in church circles, singles are singled out. It is a calling in and of itself. Maybe others don't always single us out, but maybe we single ourselves out. I am certain that God singles out those who are single for a purpose.

My heart was aching for a husband — or rather, my flesh was. I wanted a companion. I was not content in this area of my life. Elder Lynch said, "Sister Sabrina, God's going to bless you with a husband."

Don't you just hate it when people say things like that? I knew he was trying to console me, and for that I was grateful. You know how many times I had heard that? A million times! I couldn't conceal the dejectedness on my face. You would think with all the "God Talks" we have had about this area, I would be further along. However, God continued to talk to me about this matter over the years until I had contentment concerning my singlehood. Elder Lynch pulled up in my yard and let me out of the van. Before exiting, he made sure he gave me my tape.

I had driven my Nissan Altima for three years and the tape player never worked. In fact, it did not work when I purchased the car, and because the car was sold with only the power train warranty remaining, the dealership wouldn't correct it. During those three years, I listened to the radio,

88.3FM–His Radio. The season prior to this had proven to be the worst season of my life. I almost lost my life, but thank God it wasn't mine to lose and the keeper of life was keeping me in my Egypt. The bottom line: the tape player didn't work and had never worked the entire three years I had the car. I wanted to listen to songs of my choosing, but during those times God chose the songs that impacted me. Thank God for Vickie Yohe, Jaci Velasquez, and Rich Mullins. I felt "like a flower in the wind" but I knew "There Is Something About My praise."

The next day, I was getting ready to leave for work. I got in my car and I realized I had the tape in my hand. I turned my ignition on, and without even giving a thought to my non-working tape player, I placed the tape in the tape deck. All of a sudden, the music blasted through the speakers. My mouth gaped open. For a second, I didn't realize where the sound was coming from. In sheer ecstasy I was smitten, and at that instant, "God Talked." He said, "When I get ready for something to happen, it will happen, and it will happen — JUST LIKE THAT." Oh boy, did I get it. God was letting me know that when He gets ready for things to happen, they will. I don't care how long it takes. Just as He took a non-working tape player and caused it to work just like that, He will work His purposes in our lives just like that, supernatural. Three whole years and just like that, it was over. "Cast not away therefore your confidence, which hath great recompense of reward (Hebrews 10:35)."

Take The Hedge Down

I will share another "God Talk" related to my consuming desire for a husband. I was sitting at my table in my breakfast nook when it suddenly occurred to me that God was not allowing a man to even approach me. Save or unsaved, we would all like to feel that there was something attractive about ourselves. I began to have a "God Talk" about this matter. I said to the Lord, "Lord, I know I am not ugly." I went on to discuss with Him how I believed that He had a hedge about me and was not allowing me to even be approached by a suitor. This made absolutely no sense to me, since I had been praying for a husband. I asked God in that moment, during this particular "God Talk," to take the hedge down. I didn't want to be hedged in: I wanted to be found.

Well, you know the old saying? Be careful what you ask for, you just might get it. The next day when I arrived to work, a co-worker of mine called me to his office to tell me that another co-worker who was a behavior specialist was waiting in his office to meet me. He went on to tell me how he had been watching me and wanted to take me out to dinner. I was a little flattered how my "God Talk" seemed to be answered immediately, until I actually walked in his office and the gentleman was sitting at the desk waiting. He was a much older fellow. In fact, I perceived that he was about my daddy's age. I was actually dumbfounded. "God, is this a joke?" The man was very insistent that I give him the opportunity to take me out to eat. Somehow, I just couldn't stomach the possibility. I left my co-worker's office a little bewildered.

Afterwards, when I walked into my office, there was a note on my desk perched on my computer keyboard. I was a little taken aback when I picked it up and read it. Another man had stopped by my office and left the note. He said on the note he was interested in me and could I please call him? I was a little excited when I realized who it was. He was also a behavior specialist. God really has a sense of humor. I had met him about a week ago when they were touring him through the area, and they brought him to my module to explain to him how my field of expertise worked along with his discipline to help our clients meet objectives. He was a new employee. I remember thinking "wow" when he came to my classroom. He had a heavy Jamaican accent that was most intriguing!

Then the office phone buzzed and it was someone letting me know I had a call. It was him, and he expressed how he wanted to get to know me. During our conversation, I expressed how I was a church girl and very much loved the Lord. He shared with me that he would be happy to go to church with me. So we exchanged cell phone numbers and I also gave him my address. I could have melted: My "God Talk" had been answered. The hedge was down, and now just in one morning, I had two prospects. Although the first one wasn't my speed, this one seemed to prove probable.

Well, as soon as the excitement was building, my friend who had informed me about the older guy walked in. I was excited to share with him how another behavior specialist had come by my office. I noticed that as I shared with him who the guy was, he became very concerned. I was exuberant and he was spoiling my party with his countenance.

He looked at me, and he said, "Sabrina, I think that guy is married."

"You're kidding, right?"

He said, "I am certain he said he was married." So much for the party. It was over just like that. I shared with him how we exchanged information. I notice he didn't give me a home number. I called the Jamaican guy to inquire about his marriage status. His response was, "You can call it that." What? I told him that I did not date married men. He said he very much wanted to get to know me.

He said with his heavy accent, "I am attracted to you." I vehemently protested absolutely no, there is no way anything could be between the two of us. He continued to express his intent to pursue me. He did exactly that. He showed up on my area uninvited, pretending to be making rounds.

One day he showed up on my area and said, "I could just grab you and kiss you, you know." This guy was very tenacious in his pursuit. One day he even showed up at my house. No matter how I said no, he was determined.

One day I was over at security on campus, picking up keys, and he blocked the entranceway. There seemed to be no getting away from him. It was all becoming downright scary. God? I shared with my spiritual mom, Dot, how I really was trying to avoid him but he was not letting up.

Finally one day he walked up to my car and I stood up against his advances. I told him if he continued that, I would have to file a sexual harassment charge against him, especially since we were in a work environment and most of the activity was going on during work hours. He acted as if he didn't believe me, but I assured him I would. He seemed to back off after this encounter.

Well, I had a "God Talk." "God, please, God, put the hedge back up. I see what You have been keeping me from. God, put the hedge back up and keep it up."

God really makes me laugh a lot. I laugh at Him, and I am sure He laughs at me. It is funny how we can take what we want and present it to God, as if He needs a presentation from us to know what pleases us. It is funny how we will take what we want, present it to God, and expect God to bless it. Don't act as though you have never contrived your own plans and expected God to bless them. Forget about him finding me, I will find him! All I needed was for God to change His plan and make the one I was presenting to him "the one."

I told God during a "God Talk," "I don't want what You are showing me. Take it back." I told God, "He will be good enough for me."

"God Talked" and said to me, "I will not change, I will not take my word back."

I found another one. I know I wasn't fooling anyone but myself. I am sure you are asking, "Why wouldn't you just go somewhere and sit down?" Remember, all I knew was to fight. I am sure God was letting me know – "No means No."

One thing about God: He is clear when He speaks. His yeah is yeah and His nay is nay. There is no in between. God clearly told me, "He is not the one." That wasn't enough for me, so I left my front yard and went down to the church, perhaps to get a better reception. Momma always told me, "You hear what you want to hear." I lay prostrate before the Lord and I cried. I practically rolled all over the church floor. Then I heard "God Talk." "Get up and go home, I have told you all that I am going to tell you." I quickly sobered up, dried my face off, and went home. You can't force "God Talks." "My times are in thy hand (Psalm 31:15)."

You Can Do This

As much as we think we know ourselves, God knows us better. He knows everything about us. He reveals Himself. He makes Himself known more and more. He also reveals hidden things about us to ourselves. This "God Talk" is about God uncovering hidden talents that He has placed in us. He sometimes surprises us by showing us more of what He has placed in us.

I had just purchased my singlewide trailer, a twelve by sixty. It was my first home. It was a divine placement. I always tell others that God has us right where He wants us to be. If He wants us anywhere else, then we would be there. We need to learn to embrace the moment. Everything truly happens for a purpose. We might not see it at the moment, but as the old folks say, "Keep living." My daddy had encouraged me to move because he wanted someone next door to my grandmother to take care of her. My uncle wanted to sell his trailer. God had a plan. So much of my destiny was tied to this placement.

I was starting out fresh. I was trying to decorate my new place. One of my co-workers, Donna, made me a decorative broom for a house-warming gift. She shared with me that I might show it to others, and if they wanted one the price was eight dollars. It was pretty and I really liked it, but it wasn't my color. My kitchen was blue and yellow with a duck theme. I am sure if she should read "God Talks," it will be the first time that she realizes how much she contributed to my floral designing skills. God used that peach broom to unearth something within me that I had not even the slightest clue was in me.

I was sitting in my kitchen one night, trying to determine what to do with my broom when "God Talked." He said, "You can do this." That was all He said during this "God Talk." It was indeed another transforming moment for me. I went to Walmart and purchased five craft brooms and other craft materials. I came back home and went to work. I made five decorative brooms. The first one was blue and yellow and the other ones were brown. I sold all the brooms to some of my co-workers and friends. I even made a profit. I couldn't believe it, but just like that I started making all kinds of floral designs and crafts. Flowers were just as lucrative in my hands as a paintbrush. It was a new medium for me to work with. I love flowers. I have a passion for flowers, silk and fresh. God has gifted my hands. He taught me how to design.

There seemed to be nothing I couldn't do with a flower. I could tie bows and colors electrified me. I designed flowers and they sold themselves. All I had to do was show them. People were requesting my services for specialized designs. One of my co-workers, Frances Sizemore, called me one Sunday afternoon and informed me she wanted a flower arrangement for a dear friend of hers. She told me that he wasn't dead yet, but she wanted me to be prepared because they were expecting him to die at any moment. The next day she called me and told me, "He's dead now, so you can make the flower." I made a fishing boat and the fishing rod. She and so many others were really pleased with the design. She was one of my best customers. Often people would inquire as to where I went to school. I would constantly have to explain that I didn't have formal training in design from a school but from God. It was a gift from God.

God opened the door for me to teach at the Bernie Ward Community Center. Mrs. Pippin and Mr. Kelly were always pleased with the classes I taught. As a single mom, I knew God was giving me opportunity to make some money to help me. I have always thanked God for gifting me and providing opportunities so I could support my son. I taught at the community center for eight years.

I was employed as an Activity Therapist at Gracewood State School and Hospital a facility that provided services for individuals with developmental disabilities; my co-workers at Gracewood were my greatest customers. I had just had a "God Talk" about getting a part-time job. The next day after my "God Talk," Frances, one of my co-workers, called me. She told me her son, who was the manager of Michaels Arts and Craft in Atlanta, was getting ready to locate a store in Augusta and that he was interested in me because of the floral arrangements he had seen at her house. The next day I called him and applied for the floral designer position.

I got the job at Michael's Arts and Crafts. I designed there for about two years. During this season, God grew my knowledge of the names of flowers. I always signed my flowers TGBTG — that is, To God Be the Glory. I always wanted God to be glorified through the gifts He had given to me. Often customers would come in and stand at the counter and watch me design. They would often tell me that I had a gift from God. That's right, a gift from God. We never know when God will speak to us about hidden gifts.

Through the job at Michaels, I was able to participate in the 1995 Augusta Tour of Homes. I had the privilege of decorating a $400,000 house. I went on to do an exhibit at the Burke County Library. I won awards through the Burke County Fair. I stopped teaching at the community center and many of my students sought me for private lessons. I never felt threatened by teaching someone how to make floral arrangements. Some people would ask me, "You're not afraid that your students are going to take your business?" My answer was always no. After all, it was a gift to be given. Teaching my craft skills never took anything away from me, but only gave me pleasure to see others learn and enjoy my craft. I formed a lot of valuable relationships. I had students who would come from neighboring towns and South Carolina for me to teach them. One of my dearest students, Mrs. Minnie Wimfrey, would prove to be like a mother to me. She was always giving me food, extra money, and encouragement. Another one of my beloved students, who was truly an example of a woman of faith, was Brenda Davis. I watched her during the loss of her husband and she exemplified faith in action. She seemed to believe God no matter what. I admired her level of faith and I desired to have her level of faith.

I utilized my gift to give to my consumers at East Central Regional Hospital. I worked as a vocational consultant. I provided opportunities for my consumers to create floral crafts and other crafts to earn money through "The Grab-N-Go Consumer Gift Shop." Elizabeth Schoultz and Catherine Guyton, my instructors in the program, worked closely with me to help facilitate the craft groups. The consumers got to deposit the money into their accounts. For some of the consumers, this might be their only means for obtaining funds. After all, not all of them had families that were involved, and even if they did, not all of the families could afford to send their loved ones money. Thanks to Georgia State Wholesale owners and staff, who have been very generous over the years and periodically donated materials to keep this part of the program going. Thanks, Pat, Peggy and Donna. Thank You, God, for the "God Talk" that was a ministry to so many.

93

Chapter Nine

Speed Bump Ahead

"God talks"

"And when they came to the threshing floor of chidon, Uzza put forth His hand to hold the ark: for the oxen stumbled. And the anger of the Lord was kindled against Uzza, and He smote him, because he put his hand to the ark: and there he died before God. And David was displeased: because the Lord had made a breach upon Uzza: wherefore that place is called Perezuzza to this day. And David was afraid of God that day saying how shall I bring the ark of God home to me?"
~ 1 Chronicles 13:9-12

God often has "God Talks" with us in our dreams. He strengthens and warns us of many things. I have learned much through "God Talks" that occurred while I was asleep. I will share some of them as the Lord directs. When "God Talks" through dreams, we must have discernment. Not all dreams are spiritual in nature, and God does not talk through all dreams. It is imperative that we do not take every dream as spiritual, but it is equally important that we discern when God is talking to us through dreams. I receive calls all the time from those who are seeking advice concerning dreams. I am not the expert, but God is. God will establish and confirm anything that He conveys to us through "God Talks." Often it is a "wait and see," and at other times it happens instantaneously. Nevertheless, "God Talks" and "He that has an ear let him hear (Revelation 3:13)."

The Counterfeit

I had a dream one night in the year of 1997; I believe it was June of 1997. One night as I was asleep in my bed, God had a talk with me. It was as if He opened my spirit up and sealed instructions so deep within me that no matter how I would try to go the way I wanted to, those words would act as a deterrent. I have told these stories many times. This is the first time that I have written them down. God said to me during that "God Talk," "You have one more counterfeit, and then the real thing will come. It is going to look like the real thing. It is going to feel like the real thing. You are going to be closer than you have ever been. Whatever you do, do not marry him. He is a counterfeit."

Then I woke up. Those words were etched in my spirit. It wasn't until I went through this ordeal that God gave me this scripture. "In a dream in a vision of the night, when deep sleep falleth upon men, in slumbering upon the bed; Then he openeth the ears of men, and sealeth their instructions, That he may withdraw man from his purpose, and hide pride from man. (Job 33:15-18)."

At the time of the dream, I was not in a relationship. God already knows the way that we will take even before we take it. He had never talked this way to me during a "God Talk." It was new to me. I received a call from a young man whom I knew from my childhood. He wanted me to decorate his home. I will not use his name, but any of my close associates have heard this story over and over and would immediately know to whom I am referring. It was one of the biggest decorating jobs I ever undertook. He was a very pleased customer. We rekindled a friendship from our childhood. He asked my son and me to accompany him and his sons to church. Afterwards, we attended churches all the time together. I started doing other things for him during the friendship. I started cooking pancakes and other dishes. He loved my pancakes. One thing led to another, and before I knew it, one day he asked me an odd question: "Do you like me or do you hate me?"

Well, I certainly didn't hate him. What I did notice was that I had started having feelings for him. I wasn't ready to deal with the complexities of what I felt. He then expressed how he felt toward me. He gave me a plaque with a key on it, and he gave me a key and a remote to his home. On the plaque was written, "You have the key to my heart." The relationship blossomed, and before I knew it, I was in love.

He was very kind initially. Honestly, I believe he was always kind. Now that I am writing about this "God Talk," this had nothing to do with either him or me. This was about God's purpose. He said that he asked God for me.

A metamorphosis was taking place in me. Everyone around me noticed that I wasn't myself. I was not doing things that were normal for my character. I was doing things that I said I would never do. I eventually left my house and moved in with him. He would become the only man I ever lived with. I was breaking all my rules. I stopped going places, stopped doing things, stopped making flowers, stopped being with my friends, stopped going to church, and stopped calling my daddy. I was totally absorbed in my relationship with him. Dangerously, he had become my everything. Oh, did I mention I was in a state of rebellion? My daddy couldn't tell me anything. My aunt, whom I never gave a minute of trouble, couldn't tell me anything. I lost my identity; I was no longer me. It all happened so fast I couldn't see how far I had gone.

We were in his sunroom when he asked me to marry him. Every word that God spoke flooded my mind. I remember he noticed the changes in my expressions. He inquired why I looked puzzled. He assumed it was about my house that God had blessed me with. He knew about the "God Talk" about the house. Oh, what webs we weave.

He said, "Don't worry about your house, you can keep it."

I then answered him without any further delay, "Yes!" I knew all along God had said no. I had determined even at that moment not to breathe a word to him of what really troubled me. I was so deceived that I set out ambitiously trying to get God to change His Word. I pleaded with God to make this man "the one." I pleaded with God to take His Word back. During a "God Talk," God told me He would not change His Word.

I had rejected the very thing that always kept me: "God Talks." It wouldn't be my "God Talks" that saved me this time, but the "God Talks" of others like my spiritual mom, Dorothy Reid, my daddy, Reverend Joe Lewis Sr., my aunt, Pearlie Cunningham, and my dear friend, Julie Lloyd. Some days I cried out to God, "God, are You going to let the devil kill me?" I knew He was with me, but He was silent as I continued to sink deeper and deeper in sin and I knew He wasn't going to let the devil kill me. However, He was going to let me see for myself what He had already offered me, Himself, everything I needed was in Him. Sin is a bottomless pit, its depth is unknown, and I was being pulled deeper into its snare. Thank God for others who have "God Talks."

How long? I was hiding so much, or at least I thought I was. Everyone could see but me. I started planning my wedding. I bought all my flowers. He bought me the first ring I ever received from a man, and it was gorgeous. It was brilliant. I wished at the time that I had just one ray of the fire that glared at me when I looked at that marquise. Empty! My daddy fought by trying to bring correction in my life, but he soon noticed it was useless. He even offered to pay me $500 a month if I would just go home. It was useless. It wasn't about money. I had given myself wholly in this. At the time I didn't recognize it, but he had become my idol. God will not have another God before Him and He meant just that.

We had set our wedding day for February of 1998. He changed his mind and said because of his previous marriage, he would prefer another month. Well, in March he changed his mind. April, he changed his mind. He didn't change his mind about marrying me but about the timing. When I got frustrated one day, he said, "I don't know why you are getting so upset. It is the closest you have ever been."

Oh my "God Talk." He said the exact words from my dream. My life was so chaotic. One thing was for sure; I knew we needed to get back in church. We were not good for each other. We made each other sicker. We would literally spend hours staring in each other's eyes, saying, "I love you," "I love you more." I guess it was an attempt to prove something to us. I know one thing for certain: when you set out to prove you love someone, you will end up selling yourself out. The more you give, the more they require, and no matter what you do, it will never be enough. I couldn't fill his void and he couldn't fill mine.

We finally started going to church again. He was a member of his friend's church. We started attending regularly. One day the pastor preached, "Every step you make, God will honor it." It resonated within my spirit. Then "God Talked" and said, "Some things are not solved until some things are resolved." Then one night at a revival a young preacher preached a message. You would have had to hear it yourself. "Let Go of the Counterfeit, so the Real Thing Can Come."

Oh, my "God Talk," He said the exact words from my dream. I knew God was talking to me. Everything the preacher preached that night was everything I was experiencing. I looked back that night at my fiancé. I was resolute in my soul that I had to get out of the relationship with him. "God Talk" to me from a message I had heard my dad preached when I was twelve years old. My dad became a preacher long after he and my mom's turbulent divorce. When he would visit Georgia and preach at his parent's church, he would always take my siblings and myself with him. A story my dad told during one of his sermons stayed with me and I could hear so clearly the very words my dad said during his message "If I perish, I perish". I made my mind up at that moment that no matter what the risks were that I would get out of this dysfunctional relationship.

I was bound and determined no more. I might die, but I would die trying. When we got home that night, I announced I was sleeping in the guest room. I told him that I was conflicted within and I could not live the way I was living any longer. He was angry. I understood. He was hurt. I was too, but there was something inside so strong and resolute. I heard what the Spirit was saying. Eventually, I went back home. I was so worn and so belligerent. Everything was strange. The enemy tempted me with suicide one night. A very good friend of mine had committed suicide by hanging himself during this same time frame. The night I was tempted it was about 2:30 a.m. "God Talked" through a book, *Shattering the Gods Within*, by David F. Allen. God used that book to save my life. Through it, God revealed to me how narcissism works. I learned sick people make sick people sick. I saw my own rebellion that night and the price I paid, far beyond what I could even realize at that time. In many ways, even to this day, I am still paying. Only God can redeem the time lost.

I learned of a biblical character by the name of Balaam in the book of Numbers. Read the story. Boy, did God show me myself through the story of Balaam and his rebellion. We will go so long persisting in something, even when we see and know that God stands in the way against us.

Night after night would prove challenging. Some nights I sent my son to my sister, Brenda, because I didn't want him to see me this way. One night I left him in my bed and went to his room to cry. He came to his room later and caught me crying. It was one of the most touching moments in my life. My baby, for whom I sacrificed so much, raising him as a momma and a daddy, came to my rescue at just the age of seven years old. He took me by the hand and said, "Come on, Momma, I will take care of you." He led me back to my room and we went back to sleep.

The difficulty one night proved to be too much for me again, so I called my dear friend, Julie. She came in the middle of the night, traveling dark, backcountry roads. The sound of her car pulling up that night brought great relief to me. I cried, cried, and cried. In fact, for over a year I hadn't laughed. Julie overheard me still crying that night and she asked me if I wanted to get up and make some flowers.

Knowing me the way she did, she knew if anything would cheer me up, maybe making flowers would be the trick.

I looked at her and said, "I don't feel like making flowers." That was when she leaped out of the bed and said, "We need to go pray." We knelt down in my living room and she coached me through. She said, "You ask God to bring Sabrina back. You ask God to reach way down and bring her back. I don't know who this is, but I know it is not Sabrina."

I did as Julie insisted, and it worked. Day by day, I started coming back around. I was getting stronger and stronger. I still had some difficult days. I remember telling my spiritual mom during my recovery that it felt like God was holding my head under water, and I didn't mind going through because I realized what I had done, but I just wanted to catch my breath and then I would gladly go back under.

Despite the break-up, we maintained a friendship and grew to accept what the Lord was doing. It took me two whole years, but I gave him his ring back after a "God Talk," in which God asked me to. I had told my spiritual mom, "The Israelites brought the gold out of Egypt." I don't think she agreed with me, but she allowed God to handle the situation. I gave it back. He didn't want it back. He didn't ask for it back, but I did what God required of me. He became a minister at his church, and about three years later the Lord led me to start "The Heart of Jesus Church" in my home. Through the resolution of our relationship came the solution — God.

The Old Lady With Old Fire

Another time, I had a dream early in my role as a pastor. Providing pastoral service for God's people comes at a high price, and as a young pastor I had so much to learn. I still do. I was hurting. Sometimes the more you love people and give of yourself, the more they will hurt you. I thank God for longsuffering, a virtue He truly has manifested in me all my life. I love people. You can't pastor people you don't love. The Lord had me in intercessory prayer for His people.

We had experienced demonic attacks. There had been two demonic manifestations in the church, and deliverance. We also were experiencing people who were coming with an agenda to undermine what God was doing. Then add the fact that I was dealing with feelings of inadequacies because often women are looked down upon in ministry. On top of it all, I was a single woman pastor.

The Lord would often strengthen me. My spiritual mom would encourage me during these times. She reminded me of my destiny and what she could foresee God doing as I walked on. I did just that; walked on. I had a dream and "God Talked." I was in a beautiful sanctuary and an angel came to me and said, "There is an old lady and she has old fire." The angel had a hair bonnet in his hand, which he took and thrust in my stomach as he said those words. Afterwards, the angel pointed to the only other person sitting afar off on the other side and said, "There is a woman that has overcome."

I woke up, and the first question I asked God was what He meant by an old lady with old fire. I shared the dream with the congregation that day. As I was preaching during the service, all of a sudden my cousin jumped up and screamed, "Money is falling." Everyone looked around, and my Aunt Callie fell on the floor, asking her, "Where is the money?"

She violently fell to the floor and was exhibiting full body contortions. Her eyes went back in her head and they turned bloodshot red. Some of the people ran out of the sanctuary. It was only about a month ago she had been delivered from demon possession. The Lord had already told me that she went back to doing the same thing and that she was in a worse state than she was the first time. I immediately got down on the floor next to her, and Prophetess Joyce joined me praying. By now, she was foaming at the mouth. I began to do as the Holy Spirit was guiding me to do. I don't remember the exact order of how the Lord instructed me. Despite what people would have others believe, there is no set formula for deliverance. There may be similar elements during different deliverances, but there is no set way. You have to be under direction of the Holy Ghost.

The male voice that was coming from her mimicked the Lord's tongues, unlike the first time she was delivered from demons during a previous church service. I rebuked the spirit and forbade it to speak. When the Lord led me to ask it what was its name, it responded, "Lucifer." Several times during the deliverance, I looked straight in the eyes of hell and said, "I am not afraid of you."

I remember God was directing me to place my hand in different locations on her. He told me to move my hand from her stomach to her back, and then He led me to put my hand on her throat. She was still jerking and shaking until she appeared totally exhausted. Then the Lord alerted me that the demon spirit was moving around and that there was more than one. Then the Lord told me they had lodged in her throat. At that point, she appeared to be choking badly. The Lord told me I would know she was delivered because she would urinate. Her eyes were no longer all white but returned to their normal state and color where you could see her pupil. She told me, "I got to go to the bathroom." We assisted her up. She shortly came back, looking refreshed. Her eyes were still watery.

"God Talked" and told me, "Old fire is fire that has been proven and sustained over many years." Not many days after this, my spiritual mom and I went over to the house of one of her relatives, Pat. I don't quite remember why we went. I think Pat wanted Dot to come over because she had a guest at her place. When we got there, there was an older, white, petite lady who came up to greet Dot. She was excited. They hugged and exchanged a few words, then Dot turned and introduced her to me. She began to prophesy over my life.

She spoke many things. Before our visit was over, she said the Lord had told her she had to come home with me and stay with me. That little fireball did just what the Lord told her. She went everywhere I went. I had a wedding to do that Saturday and she went with me to set up. She was the most delightful woman I ever met. She was full of wisdom and God had sent her to help me. She advised me on many things during her stay. She said that Saturday night that the Lord wanted us to have a special service. She said the Lord said she had to wash everyone's feet in the church, and she did. She was also funny. She called Dot's husband, Robert, to come to church and provide music for that night. He tried to tell her that Dot and I had not spoken to him about any service, and he insisted he did not know anything about any service that night. She laughed, and said, "We didn't either." God sometimes chooses to be spontaneous, and when He does, we have to discern those moments or we will miss them. She would just go with whatever God was saying at the moment. She loved on me and encouraged me in ways I could never forget.

I shared with her the "God Talk" about the "Old lady who had old fire." She laughed and told me not to call her old. God let me know she was the old lady with the old fire. She had fire that had been proven and sustained. The devil was mad about the whole thing. She tripped over the podium and hurt her wrist, but that didn't stop her from ministering. She washed everyone's feet that night at church, including mine, and she prayed for all of us. After the service, she caught a ride back to Pat's house with Prophet Brad and Joyce.

One thing she taught me was to stop striving with my daddy about ministry and anything else. "The servant of the Lord must not strive; but be gentle unto all men, apt to teach, patient (2 Timothy 2:24)." I stopped striving with my daddy. I learned to honor my daddy and his wisdom. It wasn't long before my daddy and I were getting along again. Not long after that, my daddy came home and preached for the first time at The Heart of Jesus Church. The first night, his message was, "The Evidence Speaks for Itself." Since then, my dad has encouraged and helped me in the ministry. My daddy is an awesome man of God. I have witnessed the tremendous power of God displayed through him and I honor him.

What Do You Want?

I will share one more dream. Although there are countless times, God has used dreams to talk to me. This time, I had been providing pastoral services for about four years. I believe whatever you do, you should do it as unto the Lord. I would offer God nothing short of my absolute best. Some people are in ministry and some people are given to ministry. I was a person completely absorbed in whatever God was asking of me. God has taught me balance along the way. I could be over-zealous at times, even religious, but "God Talked" to me in a dream.

In the dream, my son and I were in the Heart of Jesus churchyard. There were huge snakes positioned all around the church. They were in different positions. Some were stretched out straight and others were curled up. One thing God revealed to me in the dream was that all the snakes were dead. They didn't look dead, but they were. My son, Rardietrick was standing on the porch of the church. As I saw him bend over to pick up the huge snake on the porch, I screamed, "Don't pick that snake up, he might be playing dead." I watched in dismay as my words didn't reach him in time and he lifted the huge reptile up. Amazingly, as I watched, the whole snake crumbled and fell apart in his hand.

Then I woke up. I knew God was definitely warning me of some danger, but whatever it was it would fall apart. Some things God warns us of, we may be steered around by providence, and others He may just allow us to go through. In either case, we should be engaging in "God Talks."

A week later on a Sunday morning, I needed to go to the laundromat to dry some clothes before church. At that time, our services didn't start until 2:30 p.m. My washing machine was working but my dryer wasn't. Usually Dee would stay home until I went and came back, but this time he wanted to follow me. He was twelve at the time. So, he went with me this particular morning. While at the laundromat, he asked me if he could walk over to the store. Since it was in close proximity and he had done it countless times before, I gave the okay.

Well, it wasn't a good fifteen minutes and I saw the policeman's car driving up with my child in the back seat. I didn't have a clue as to what was going on. I met the police outside. He walked up to me and asked me if this was my son. I could see Dee crying in the back seat. My heart sank. That was a sight for any mother to see, my baby! The officer explained to me that I needed to follow him to the police station. He explained to me Dee had walked out of the store with a magazine concealed in his coat. I couldn't believe it. My baby had never stolen anything. If he wanted something, he always asked for it. Thank God, my clothes were finished. I gathered them quickly and threw them in the car. I followed him to the station.

I was so upset. I couldn't believe this was happening to me. I had a "God Talk" all the way to the jail. I was hurt, embarrassed, angry, and all kinds of emotions were going through me. "God," I said, "I am so busy taking care of Your people, tell me who is taking care of my son?" I cried and sobbed until I pulled up to the jail. The Lord strengthened me.

The police threatened to take Dee to a youth detention center. Since there was no prior incident, he told me he could release him into my custody. It was getting late, by then it was almost 12:30 p.m., and everything that was going through my head was aimed to get us out of there. I would have a church service in the next two hours. He finally let us go. Not without informing me that Dee would have to go to a hearing and Dee would have a record the rest of his life that would follow him.

This was painful. I was angry at Dee. I cried, yelled, and wept. It was like the end of the world for me. Dee was visibly upset and extremely apologetic. He seemed lost for words to comfort me. The enemy taunted me, "How are you going to preach today? What can you tell God's people? You can't control your own twelve-year-old son." In tough times, God carries His people. By His grace, I got ready for church. I had shared the dream with the church the week before. When I got to church, I shared what had just happened with Prophetess Joyce, Brad, Frieda, and others. They were all encouraging me.

Then Prophetess Joyce said, "Pastor, God said no weapon formed against you and Dee will prosper." As she spoke the "God Talk," the dream came back to me. The snakes were already dead. When Dee picked the snake up in the dream, it fell apart. The Lord used me mightily that day. The truth is, when we are weak, God is strong. God chooses to demonstrate His power in broken vessels.

That night I cried before God. I lay prostrate on the floor next to my bed all night. I had a "God Talk" all night. "Lord," I cried, "he is my son, my only son." The enemy will use the closest thing to us to hurt us. For me, it was my son. I was sharing what had happened with Pastor Bing, my son's god-father, my daddy, my spiritual mom, Dot, and all my family. Everyone assured me that they would be talking to God.

I disciplined Dee over and over. I wanted to make sure he would never go this way again. My son tried to make it up to me by offering to pay for my gas on one occasion with money my dad had given him. When he did, I realized he didn't owe me anything and I knew he was sorry. I knew he didn't mean to do anything to hurt me. I was just taking this so personally, because I felt that with all I gave in ministry to God's people,

that God would exempt me from such pain. I labored hard —
beyond 100 percent. I understood deep within that God would
vindicate me and my baby, and God would have the last laugh.
I was just taking this to heart. What the enemy meant for harm,
God would turn it for our good.

Everyone had offered to go and support us when Dee had
his hearing. Pastor Bing told me to make sure I called him.
However, when the time came, God instructed me not to call
anybody. The morning of the court hearing for my son, I had
a "God Talk." He said, "What do you want?" Before I could
give it a thought, what was in my heart came out. I told God,
"I want it to be like this never even happened."

Nothing is too hard for God. I went to work that day
without a care in the world. I had arranged to leave work early
to give myself enough time to pick Dee up from school and
get to the hearing on time. I picked him up. I resented even
having to go through this. I started telling him, if he hadn't
done this we wouldn't be going to the hearing. My son sat
quietly in the back seat. Then "God Talked," "Don't you see
he is hurting? What you do now is going to make a difference
in the rest of his life."

I parked the car, and grabbed my baby's hand and we had a
"God Talk." Afterwards we went into the building. I didn't know
what to do, so I checked with the receptionist. She instructed
us to sign in and have a seat. I began to minister to her while
we were waiting. She started crying and said, "Ma'am, God
sent you in here today." Then we were called to the back for
the hearing. The young man conducting the hearing knew us.
God was at work. The young man talked to Dee for about fifteen minutes. He then turned to me and said, "Miss Lewis, I
don't see the need to go any further, this will be like it never
happened. Get your son and go home." Oh, my "God Talk."
Exactly what I told God. We never heard any more from that
young man. We went away praising God over and over again
for His faithfulness. What an awesome God we serve!

God Talks at the Chapel

We are creatures of habit in many things, but I have found developing the habit of having "God Talks" is not only cathartic for you, but it is critical to the plan and will of God to be facilitated in others' lives. Sometimes the urgency of the moment presses us beyond the norm into the miraculous display of God's power. By virtue of the friendship established with God through habitual communion with Him, "God Talks." As King Solomon said, "I have seen many things under the sun," and so have I.

At my job, there was a group of ladies who met every Wednesday to have "God Talks." I became a part of this group through my spiritual mom, Dorothy. The group had been meeting faithfully for many years. Sometimes the size of the group dwindled to only a few members, but over the years my spiritual mom and I had consistently continued to have "God Talks" no matter the circumstances.

We had designated our lunchtime for having "God Talks," but sometimes we had to alter the time and seize the moments given us. We had designated the campus chapel as a meeting place, but often our meeting place became our cars, the park behind the building we worked in, my office, my classroom — you get the point. We not only grew in our relationship with God, but also with each other. We were a prayer team and had faithfully been given to intercessory prayer for about seventeen years. Over the years, many had joined us.

I cannot go further without remembering the faithful pioneer of this prayer ministry: Sister Juanita Johnson. Her vision and faithfulness in this endeavor started something great. Another sister I remember very vividly during those years was Sister Nancy Reese. Many years of communication that took place every Wednesday solidified a forging of pride in my soul, when after these pioneers retired, their mantle fell on me. What a privilege and honor was bestowed upon me.

Throughout "God Talks," you may observe many accounts where my spiritual mom is often mentioned, and that in itself reveals the role she has played in "God Talks." Again, thank God for good spiritual discipline that becomes habitual. The strategic thing about talking to God through "God Talks" is that He gives us the opportunity to come to Him and He shows us things to come, often preparing us in advance. Power bursts forth in these moments and the momentum is strikingly different than at other times. These are opportune times for God's intervention through the power of His anointing. The presence of God's power is so tangible that the very hairs on your body stand erect. His presence is undeniable: it ruffles the atmosphere and pierces the soul. Oh how true it is that no one can do you like Jesus. Every time we met, we had such encounters: At all times it was through the roof!

We often interceded in response to oppressions and injustices that were practiced at the hospital facility where we worked. Many employees would cry out for intercession and often would come to the chapel for prayer. It was a ministry sphere that God had placed us in for the tyranny that Satan would display through wickedness and injustice in some management positions. Weak and feeble people had been victimized. Several people in positions of authority acquired a reputation for ruthless dealings, although they might have identified themselves as Christians. I am sure you know of such individuals and their bullying spirit that terrorizes people into fear and submission. HSTs (Human Service Technicians) direct care staff, so the backbone of personal care was often oppressed.

All Authorities Derive Their Authority From The Lord

We continued to have "God Talks" on behalf of the oppressed, for tyranny is unbearable. One thing for sure, we must refuse to let fear dominate us. We must continue to be proactive through "God Talks."

As David said when he was overwhelmed, I asked the Lord, "When my heart is overwhelmed, lead me to the rock that is higher than I" (Psalm 61:2). I had battle fatigue from the constant battling, but God had me remain fierce in the face of the opposition and He also continuously ministered to me abundantly, teaching my hands to war (Psalm 18:34).

One day as we were having a "God Talk," God talked and said to me that all authority derives its authority from Him and there was no one in authority that He had not placed. He let me know that day — be it good or bad, He expected me to submit myself. I was obedient, and instead of being absorbed with my complaint concerning the oppression, I understood that God was allowing it in that season. What I didn't see from my limited perspective was that God was working everything together for my good — "And we know that all things work together for good to them that love God, to them that are called according to his purpose" (Romans 8:28).

A year earlier, "God Talked" and woke me up out of my sleep at 3:00 a.m. and said, "For promotion cometh neither from the east, nor the west, nor from the south" (Psalm 75:6). Shortly afterwards, the position for activity therapist supervisor became available. I interviewed for it but it was unjustly awarded to my intern, despite my seventeen years of exceptional service. News of the injustice inundated the campus, and many were outraged and urged me to file a grievance. "God Talked," and said no. The same woman who brought terror to so many was behind this injustice and soon became my direct supervisor. In the midst of it all, God was still requiring submission and trust.

A Leper In The King's Court

We just need to be able to trace the providential hand of God, and what appears to be chaos will take on a form that clearly reveals that God is in control. There was some downsizing in the state of Georgia, due to budget shortfalls. Two state hospitals were to be merged into one, which would mean that duplicate managerial positions would be collapsed into one and those that occupied those positions had to compete for their position. It was during this same time that "God Talked" — "I have placed a leper in the king's court to restore unto you what was lost." He gave me the reference scripture and the story of the Shunammite woman restored in 2 Kings 8:1-6. Gehazi, the servant who had served Elijah, was a leper and was considered unclean. However, he was in the king's court with the king when the Shunammite woman returned after the famine that Elijah had warned her of.

When she returned, God had Gehazi in the right place at the right time, although according to custom he should not have been in the king's court because he was a leper and considered unclean. Nevertheless, he was there. The king inquired about the great things that Elisha had done, and as he was telling the king how Elisha restored a woman's son to life, at the same time the woman was inquiring for her house and land. Gehazi identified her as the woman unto whom the miracle was done. The king appointed an officer to restore all that was hers. "God Talked," and let me know He would place someone out of their element to restore to me what was lost.

Sure enough, the woman my current boss had to compete against for her position, not coincidentally but amazingly and providentially was the same woman under whom my professor at Georgia Southern College would not allow any interns from the college to do their internship, because he said she was a racist and he had to withdraw students from the intern program. Well, my current boss competed for her position but didn't get the job. Instead, the woman my college professor had warned me about years ago became my new boss. The enemy truly was all around me, but God was at work!

The hospital then offered my former boss, my friend Linda, another position. We were therapeutic recreation specialists by trade and degree. Client employment was a different element for my former boss, and she almost didn't accept the position. She was very hurt through the whole process, but God placed her there in her new position, as He had said. She had been the buffer for me in my distress. Also in the middle of all this, it became apparent that God had preserved me by not allowing me to get the position that was given to my intern, because in the middle of this downsizing, they phased out that position. Had I been in that position, I would have been without a job. Praise God! It was all coming together!

Sure enough, my cry was as Habakkuk, "How long, O Lord shall I cry?" I continued to cry out to God and submit in the process to whatever I was asked to do. My obedience was unto Him and I honored those who were in authority over me. God had talked concerning my situation and all I had to do was be obedient. My former boss told me of a possible position that was in the process of being created, and she also informed me of a possible opening in her new department. She explained to me about her new job and how she was enjoying it. God truly prospered her no matter what she did. She could take the theories of practice and apply it in her new position. She encouraged me to apply for both positions and that was all she could share with me. She was honorable and would not in any wise allow her personal friendship to interfere with her professional judgment. Therefore she encouraged me to apply for both, and if I didn't get the position with her, perhaps the other one would work out.

The enemy will always try to counterfeit the works of God. I was offered the other position, but there was such a demonic presence with that offer, I couldn't take it. The other offer came with a spirit of confusion. I had to call my spiritual mom to pray with me. From that Friday night to Sunday night, I was under attack. My soul was in stress. I almost canceled my interview with my former boss and the interview panel for the position in her department, and just in the moment of time, "God Talked." I realized there was something amiss with the manager who had presented the other opportunity. Late that night, I sought counsel of my daddy and my friend – my former supervisor. There was a spirit of agreement between my daddy and my former boss, so I went to my interview as scheduled.

I did exceptionally well with the interview and I got the job. Praise God, after seventeen years in one building – in the same position — I got the job. What a thrill it was. God provided me a way of escape – He delivered me from the hands of my enemy. He had fulfilled yet another "God Talk." The restoration was beyond what I could have imagined at the time. Prior to me getting my new position in Work Therapy, the woman my professor had warned me about years ago had wrongfully received a donation of floral supplies that were intended for me to receive on behalf of the hospital. She not only took the donation of floral supplies but she distributed them at her own discretion and held back most of the flowers so that what I received for my department was very meager. Adding insult to injury, neither she nor her staff knew what to do with the flowers, so she had the audacity to asked my new boss if I could come in-service her and the staff on how to use the materials. Well, my boss would not permit that. God is awesome!

God had given Prophetess Joyce, one of the members of the Heart of Jesus, a Word of Knowledge concerning me prior to all of these occurrences. She said, "Pastor, I see keys in your hand." Well, indeed, I was given keys to my new building, which was on the other campus. It was a new beginning. I was excited, because I had been with the mental retardation population for seventeen years and now I would be working with the population I interned with, mental health and forensics in the expansion of the work therapy program to the hospital's sister campus.

Let me tell you what I discovered in my new building — you might have to take your seat! All the flowers that were taken from me a year ago were locked in a storage area in my new building! It was indeed like a dream. Not only that, I was supposed to receive only a five percent raise with the new position because it was a just a pay grade above my current pay grade, but God granted me ten percent, equivalent to the raise I would have received if I had got the other position that I had waited for and felt that I was cheated out of. Another "God Talk" fulfilled!

In the midst of our going through repeated trials and tribulations, things can wear heavily upon us and we might be surprised how even when we think we are okay, we could be very affected by what we have gone through. I recall how one day at home in my breakfast nook, I shook in total awe of my confession of not liking the individual who came to our building as our manager. "God Talked" and told me to submit. "Oh, my God," I confessed, "I don't like her." It stunned me. I loved her, but I didn't like her, and even that was horrifying for me to exclaim, for with all that I am, I love people. I immediately called my spiritual mom and told her of this discovery. In her calm, sweet voice, she said, "I know." She recounted to me her own experience in this area, as she too had admittedly along the way had this same confession about another person on the job.

What does one do with such revelation? Have a "God Talk." In the same minute that I open my mouth with that confession, I also open my mouth to tell Him, and immediately

I experience such an awareness of His presence that I am overcome with the grace that was released in my spirit at that very moment. I pitied the soul of that woman. I amazingly softened to see the woman in which the spirit of Leviathan was manifesting himself. Oh, how I thank God for pulling that thorn out of my spirit.

On my way to work the next day as I traveled Highway 25 North, I had a "God Talk," where the fruit of His amazing grace fragrantly filled my car as I pleaded for her to keep her job in the downsizing, because her position was on the chopping block. One thing I learned for sure was "God Talked," "But where sin abounded, grace did much more abound" (Romans 5:20).

Chapter Ten

Charting New Territories

"God talks"

"Now when they had gone throughout Phrygia and
the region of Galatia, and were forbidden of the Holy
Ghost to preach the word in Asia. After they were come
to Mysia they assayed to go into Bithynia but the Spirit
suffered them not. And passing by Mysia came down to
Troas. And a vision appeared to Paul in the night; There
stood a man of Macedonia and prayed him saying,
Come over into Macedonia and help us. And after he
had seen the vision, immediately we endeavored to go
into Macedonia, assuredly gathering that the Lord had
called us for to preach the gospel unto them."
~ Acts 16:6-10

He Will Be With You

God often sends angels in our midst. It was not uncommon to me, for He had done so on several occasions as recorded in several "God Talks." We were having Bible study at the Heart of Jesus Church one night. We always looked for an encounter with God every time we entered, and without fail, He has always met us. This particular night a very aged white man, who appeared to be utterly poor, his clothes looked worn-straggly, entered our midst. The word of God tells us to be careful how we entertain strangers, for many have entertained angels unaware (Hebrews 13:2). Although you could not help noticing his outward appearance, his presence was regal. Service was already in process. He didn't say anything when he first entered. In fact, I don't recall him saying anything until the end of service, when we inquired about his name.

He entered and went to the back of the church and bowed down with his face to the floor in a corner. At times he raised his hands to heaven and worshipped the Lord throughout the service. At the end when we inquired to know his name, he told us his name was "John," and that was it. So we called him, "Mr. John." He gave out paper checks that stated, "For God so loved the world, that he gave his only begotten Son, that whosoever believeth in him should not perish, but have everlasting life (John 3:16)." We discerned that Mr. John was no mere man. His countenance was very peculiar. He stated how the name of the church captivated him so much that he came to see it, "The Heart of Jesus." He said little else that night and left without further explanation of who he was. The next Wednesday he showed up for Bible study. This time he entered, stood up in our midst, and began to prophesy great things concerning The Heart of Jesus Church. He spoke of the greatness of a place that bore the name of Jesus. He spoke of the great things that God would do through the ministry. He also spoke of the love that filled the place. During offering time, he came to the altar and emptied both of his pockets in the basket. He passed out more of the checks with John 3:16 on them. This time, we all walked out together and noticed he was driving a very beat up old blue Grand Am. He didn't tarry but left. We were mystified by the aura that surrounded Mr. John. He indeed was more than a man. We all were in one accord when it came to that. The experience was so surreal and we waited for the next encounter with expectancy.

Our wait wasn't long. I should say *my* wait wasn't long, for what we didn't know was when he visited that week that it would be his last visit to us corporately. I was coming down Highway 25 from work. I was always hurrying. My schedule didn't allow for lingering. I had to pick my son up from school by 5:00 p.m. I got off work at 4:30 p.m. The drive from Augusta to Waynesboro was a thirty-minute drive uninterrupted. There was a chill in the air that day and I knew I had to stop at the church to turn the heater on so the church wouldn't be cold during Bible study. I was on the move. Hey, you do the math. I came rushing down the highway, my mind completely absorbed with all that I had to do in the time frame I had to do it in.

When I made it to the church, I noticed Mr. John's car was parked on the side of the highway along the wood line. I marveled at his being so early because I knew he knew we didn't start until 7:30 p.m. Unfortunately, as much as I wanted to stop, time just wouldn't allow me to. I waved almost frantically to hopefully alert him to his error in timing. He smiled and waved back. When I unlocked the gate to the church and pulled into the churchyard, he didn't follow. I ran inside, set the thermostat, and made a dash back to my car and out the gate. I hurried along to make it to Waynesboro. I waved again, in hopes that he understood and would come back later. I was bamboozled! Everything in me just wanted to stop, but I knew I had to go. I even looked back through my rear view mirror at him. He was still there.

Then "God Talked." "You see him now, but you will not see him anymore, but he will be with you." I let out a gasp in dismay of it all. He really was an angel, just as we knew. His name lingered on my lips, Mr. John.

Immediately a peace filled my heart. I slowed down. Suddenly I felt like I had all the time in the world. God was redeeming it for me. I could take my time. I knew I would be on time to get Dee. Funny, when I arrived at the school, I had to wait about fifteen minutes for Dee. That night at Bible study, I told everyone what God had said during our "God Talk." They all marveled. We knew God had graced us with an experience for a lifetime. We had hugged and prayed for an angel. We thought we were giving him something, but he was giving us something, An Encounter.

After church, we noticed as we walked out that there was a note wrapped around a cassette tape over the light globe on the porch. It was from Mr. John. I can't remember what the note said exactly, and since then despite all my efforts to keep the note and the tape, they seemed to have vanished. I could only believe God didn't want the church or me to make a shrine of the articles. I do remember the content of the note was inspiring, as if to say, "You are on the right track, stay the course," and the tape was a tape from Kenneth Copeland Ministry. The tape was about the Challenger Disaster, the space shuttle that exploded in the air and the astronauts who died aboard. I can vaguely remember that it dealt with the fear of death. I often wondered why John had left that particular tape and why was it something from Kenneth Copeland Ministry. I often wonder what the significance, if any, was. I did know that one day while watching Gloria Copeland teach, God used her to confirm my pastoral calling. In fact, it was while watching her teaching that God gave me the name for the church, "The Heart of Jesus." The Spirit of the Lord filled my house and the Shekinah Glory congealed like a mist surrounding me as "God Talked."

I also reflected on my childhood friend named Mr. John, and pondered whether the angel Mr. John had anything to do with my friend Mr. John. When I was little, I used to think he looked like a squirrel. He always gravitated to me more than to the other children in the neighborhood. He always said I was special, set apart, and would pat me on the head and give me a nickels and sometimes quarters. Now, I am not saying he wasn't fond of other children in the neighborhood, but he always said I was special. He would often tell me that one day, he would be dead and gone, but I would remember what he said, it would come back to me. His words have often come back to me. He wasn't the only one who often pulled me aside and told me I was special. Mrs. Sarah, one of my old friends frequently would call me from running and playing with the other children in the neighborhood to sit with her on her front porch. She told me I was different, and one day when she would be dead and gone, I would see what she meant by that. I am certain that Mrs. Sarah and Mr. John spoke by providence.

I would look daily for Mr. John to come walking down the rocky dirt road along the railroad track. One day he didn't come as he always did daily. Then rumor surfaced in the neighborhood that some mad man had stabbed him multiple times, trying to rob him, and he was dead. I was overcome with grief. I was about eight years old at the time. My dearest friend, Mr. John — it was true. He was the first of my older friends to depart. He was harmless and so gentle. One could only ponder what would drive anyone to hurt such a dear old fellow. I couldn't tell my story without telling his. Mr. John, the angel, brought back fresh memories of my childhood friend Mr. John. Now, I had assurance that though Mr. John was taken away from me, Mr. John, the angel, would be with me. "God Talked!"

You're Getting Ready to Fly

I was walking across campus at work and "God Talked" and said, "Look up, you're getting ready to fly." Fly, Lord? I had always said that I would never get on anybody's plane. I was afraid of flying. I was suddenly engulfed in a sense of peace that I was indeed about to fly somewhere soon.

A few weeks later, a pastor friend of mine called me, Elder Dairsow, and asked me to be the speaker on opening night of the Women At The Well Conference in Bridgeton, New Jersey. She told me she would be putting me down for the first night of the conference. She also informed me she would be making my flight arrangements. She was certain that God would give me a word in season. "God Talked" — He told me I was getting ready to fly, and just like that it manifested. Pastor Sabrina Lewis is getting ready to do something she never had done, and that was fly.

I was preoccupied with anticipation of what it would feel like to be on a plane. I had a lot of questions. I knew if God required me to do this ministry assignment that I could rest assured He would take care of me. I pondered if I would bail out when I got to the moment. I knew I couldn't. After all, God had opened this door for me. I was relieved somewhat when Deacon Otis agreed that his wife, Minister Annette could accompany me as my companion. Now, the question was what message did God have for Bridgeton, NJ.

Elder Dairsow was certain that God would give me a word in season. I could remember when I met her about two years earlier that God had divinely connected us. I met her at one of her conferences in Swainsboro, Ga. I remembered during her first conference I attended, I sat in the audience. I was asked at the end of the conference to share a word. I shared how "God Talked," and said, "Therefore say unto them, Thus saith the Lord God; There shall none of my words be prolonged any more, but the word which I have spoken shall be done, saith the Lord God (Ezekiel 12:28)."

The next day, I was in Augusta, Ga at one of my favorite spots — Goodwill. I received a phone call that Elder Dairsow was requesting my presence in Swainsboro, Ga. She wanted to meet with pastors and other leaders in the area. I hesitated for a moment until I heard "God Talk," "Don't miss your moment." I was still exhausted from being in last night's service in Swainsboro, so I called Minister Annette to see if her husband would release her to go, and sure enough he did. She drove me to Swainsboro where we had the leaders meeting.

I remember this mighty woman of God leaned toward me and said, "Pastor Sabrina, don't be afraid to connect." I know God had to reveal it to her because I was extremely cautious – downright leery of connecting with other people in the ministry. However, from the minute "God Talked" and spoke those words to me through her, I became at ease. This would later become one of the most pivotal relationships in my destiny. She has a prophetic administrative anointing and she has spoken many things into my life over the years. Now God was using her to introduce me to a new platform.

Three Minutes

It was not coincidental that I had just made my initial trip to Bridgeton when the mother of my church died. I made the trip with her family for the Home Going Service. Sometimes

125

pastors incur various hurts through ministry that are unconscionable. I had labored with Momma Marie throughout her
illness. I often would visit her throughout her health ordeal.
She was a powerful praying mother. I know she often prayed
for me. She had such confidence in my walk with God. Even
during her crisis, she encouraged me many days when she
called to check on me. We had such a strong bond. So there
seemed to be no question that I would eulogize her. So when
I was told another pastor would be doing so, I was completely distraught. I was even more hurt by the time that I
would be given to speak some words of comfort at her funeral.
Honestly, I was so hurt. I didn't know why this affected me
so deeply. I couldn't put a term to the depths of what I was
feeling, until one day I shared the incident with a friend of
mine, Minister Marvin, and he called it dishonor. I was told
I had three minutes to speak at Mother Marie's funeral and
despite the disappointment of not having more time, I was
determine to abide by the wishes of her daughter. There are
two "God Talks" I would like to share concerning this season.

The first is that we were in church service at The Heart
of Jesus Church and "God Talked" and told me in the midst
of the service that we were to stop and go have church with
Momma Marie at her bedside. We all spontaneously left the
church at God's bidding and went to Momma Marie and
Brother Monk's place. When we arrived, there seemed to
be some question as to whether she could receive us or not.
When she learned that it was her church family, she gave
permission gladly to receive us. She was overjoyed to have
us. She was very strong and courageous, as she always was.
She praised God and sang along with us, lifting up the name
of Jesus through thanksgiving. Not one complaint came
out of her mouth. She gave God glory. She demonstrated a
resolve that in her final hours she would glorify God. This
would be her last church service with her church family. Now
that I think about it, she must have made her request known

unto God, "Just give me one more opportunity to be in Your house," and He brought the House to her. There we all were around her bedside. She hugged and kissed us all, but she lingered with me even longer.

This would become the moment that would highlight the three minutes I was given to speak at her home going. Not even cancer could stop her praise. Not even morphine could stop her praise! The other "God Talk" I recall is one night while I was sitting at my breakfast nook table. Because of the hurts, I was contemplating not going to New Jersey. Sometimes when "God Talks," He doesn't say a word. All of a sudden, I was totally consumed and blanketed with joy beyond description. I could only inquire, "What is this?" All my hurts vanished like thin air. I could not feel any more pain, not even a residue. This blanket of joy landed swiftly and softly upon me and I was so comforted. I remember crying out in ecstasy, "Oh God, if only Pastor Evelyn and Brother Monk could feel this." I wished that they could even get a fraction of what I felt right then. Pastor Evelyn was Momma Marie's daughter and Brother Monk was her husband of forty-plus years. They were going through their own hurts. I remember, that same night I had to travel to the Walmart in Waynesboro to pick up some items I needed for the trip to Jersey. As I traveled, Sister Stephanie and I prayed and magnified God so over the phone to a place of other dimensions. I was leaping and shouting and praising God and was so submitted to whatever God required of me in this season.

It was awesome! I was only given three minutes by the family to speak. I was humbled and did accordingly. God used those three minutes of words of comfort and summed up the life of a dear matriarch in the faith. So many people thronged me that day. One man said to me concerning the pastor who eulogized her, "We heard him but we felt you." This would be another whole "God Talk" if I got into this, but let's just say, God was glorified. Mother Marie had told everybody in that city about The Heart of Jesus Church family. There were people constantly walking up to me throughout the repast, telling me how much she had shared with them about her love for her pastor and her church family. She was a prayer warrior – always "Talking to God." She lived a life of prayer. Elder Dairsow was comfort and support to me throughout this ordeal.

Strengthen That Which Remains

Now I would be going back to Bridgeton, NJ. The same place that Mother Marie funeral was. This time I would fly and this time I was going to preach. I had many "God Talks" about the message He would have me preach. During this time, my son was going through some pretty rough times at school. It was his senior year. He had always been smart in school. We had some trying moments and there were times it appeared that he was shutting down at the end. He wasn't applying himself and he was just doing anything to get by. I was absolutely baffled at how he would wait until the end of the school term, at the time of his graduation to not put forth his best effort to graduate.

I had gone to the school to talk with the counselors. They expressed to me that he was in college prep classes and could not convert this late in the school term to vocational prep. They told me at the rate things were going, it would be nowhere possible for him to graduate. At this time, I was just fed up with Burke County High School. They told me he could possibly do it if he attended Saturday school, which was designed to help students make up missing assignments. He had passed the graduation test his junior year but just needed to finish out the curriculum.

I had a "God Talk" in regards to this matter. I just told God, "I want him out of Burke County High School." He appeared to be oblivious to all my encouragement. I continued to have "God Talks" about the matter. I was in a Friday night service one night before I had to take him to Saturday school. During the Saturday night service, a young lady prophesied to me that God wanted me to lay prostrate before Him more. I almost resented what she said because I stayed on my face before God. When I took my son to school the next day. I let him out of the car at the back of the building and then "God Talked," " Get out and lay prostrate before Me." I looked around and I drove on around the school. When I got to the front of the school, "God Talked" to me again, "You want him out, get out and lay prostrate before Me." The funny thing was that if I had done it in the back, I would not have to risk the embarrassment of someone seeing me and thinking I might be crazy. When I missed that opportunity, I found myself in front of the school, facing the highway. I would not have cared who saw me at that point. I jumped out of my car facing the highway and lay prostrate on the asphalt as if it was cotton down. I knew the instant I was obedient, it was done.

I continued to increase my time lying prostrate before the Lord. One night, "God Talked," and told me to go lay before Him at 3:00 in the morning. As I lay before Him that morning, He told me, "I am not going to send you to New Jersey empty-handed." He spoke the message that I was to speak in Jersey, "Strengthen That Which Remains: There is still life in you." He even showed me how the man who the Good Samaritan assisted was half-dead. I had never seen a scripture that had the phrase "half-dead," but there was still life (Luke 10:25-37). God even showed me through this word how not to focus on what my son was doing wrong, but "Strengthen What Remained." Oh God, I began to encourage the good I saw in my son. "Behold to obey is better than sacrifice, and to hearken than the fat of rams (1 Sam. 15:22)."

Remember, the school counselors said there was no way my son could graduate, and he had been college prep and there was no way he could change from it. Well, "God Talked." He not only graduated but he received both seals

— college and tech prep! I was excited. I knew that this would be a testimony I would include in my message in New Jersey.

We were off to the Hartsfield International Airport in Atlanta, Georgia, to fly into Philadelphia, Pennsylvania. My first flight! I was quite comical. I had to laugh at myself! I was extremely grateful for my traveling companion. She knew exactly what to do. I would have been utterly lost. They checked our bags in, and we went through all the security measures. Everything was done at such a rapid pace. The only thing going through my mind was, "I have come too far to chicken out! God just help me make the leap. Maybe close my eyes and it will be all over." People looked like they were being herded around like cows. A train whipped us to some other area where we went through even more checks. I was thinking, "Wow!"

We finally ended up at our terminal and waited for them to call us to get on the plane. I was mesmerized by all the activity, but every thought in my head was, "Lord, don't let me chicken out!" As we sat waiting, we were talking to others who were waiting. I assured everyone that it was my first flight and that the only reason I was there was to go to a preaching engagement, and had Jesus not required me to do so, I wouldn't be near an airport. The bottom line was: This is what God has required of me, so here I am. I laughed. I was only making sure that if I chickened out, all the onlookers would understand! Funny, how God compels you to go on when everything seems to be collapsing within. It seemed as if everyone around me had to hear my story. Perhaps I was looking for assurance and just about everybody was giving me support.

Down the long hallway, and onto the plane, "Here I am, God. God? Oh, there You are!" Jesus was on the plane with me! The pilot and flight crew gave instructions, and there were televisions in front of every seat, playing instructions. I was sure not to miss one detail, as if my life depended on it.

We were midway along the plane, like near the wings. After I overheard some people saying that we were in the best seats, I was further relieved. They said if we were in the back, we could hear the engines. I sure didn't want to hear anything. Some told me it would feel like a car ride and others told me I wouldn't feel anything at all. Off we went: Take-off time. At first it did feel like a car ride, until it lifted off the ground. The front of the plane pointed upward. I didn't like the feeling. Annette assured me that once we got in the air, the plane would level off. Well, that seemed to take forever. I buried myself in a book, trying to escape my present reality until it finally leveled off. Then I noticed an attendant with a cart and they made some more announcements. By the time they rolled the cart down the aisle and back up the aisle, everyone had gotten snacks, the best little cookies in the world, the plane was descending. I looked out of the windows and the beauty of the heavens was stunning. It looks like God just sat us against the backdrop of heaven. Then I noticed what appeared to look like the earth! I almost didn't recognize it. For the first time in my life, I was seeing the earth from a whole new perspective. The plane was descending. Then all of a sudden it felt like the plane was bumping against something, like it was hitting something. I was slightly alarmed. No, I was really alarmed. I was shocked that others were not concerned. They continued their activity as if it was nothing. I phoned my son and shared with him about the plane and the bumping. He laughed at me and said "Momma, that's just turbulence. Are you scared?" I responded, "No, I am not scared." An announcement came over the speakers, asking people to turn off their cell phones. Annette told me that normally when the plane experiences that amount of turbulence, the pilot would normally come on and say something to the passengers. She assured me everything was fine and that the turbulence was a result of the plane descending through the clouds. I relaxed some and soon we were on the ground. Glory to God: I made it!

Dairsow had one of her assistants named Joy pick us up from the airport and drive us to Bridgeton, NJ. She was quite a jewel, extremely pleasant. We arrived at our hotel in Vineland, NJ. The two towns were in close proximity. We got settled in and that evening, another sister by the name of Erica picked us up for church. What a night God would prove! It was a mighty move of God, the first night of the conference. "God Talked," "Strengthen that which remains: There is still life in you." People thronged me, so many people surrounded me. I had ascended into the dimensions of Heaven. I remember after the benediction, people still sat in the sanctuary, gazing on the glory. Many expressed that they could not move. They were serving food across from the church in the social hall, but it would seem like an eternity before we could leave the sanctuary because so many lingered that night and for such a long time. There was much talk about that night, of how the glory of God enveloped His people. God wanted Bridgeton to know that there was still life in them and they needed to strengthen what remained.

Prior to my coming to Bridgeton for this engagement, I was informed by our lienholder for the church property that he was divorcing his wife and that I needed to direct the property payment to him. I was concerned about what was going on with them, because I knew it was with his wife that I had found favor in regard to the sale of the property. We had leased the property for about five years, until one day in 2007, I ran into his wife at Taylors Barbecue in Waynesboro, Ga. She said she had been looking for me. She asked if I was ready to purchase the property. I was stunned as to how that could be. She went on to tell me that they would owner finance with no money down on a $100,000 loan. She shared with me that our payment would not be much more than what we paid for rent and the term of the loan would be fifteen years. My aunts, Callie and Virginia, were with me. We began rejoicing at what God was doing on behalf of the church. A blessing will not only find you but it will overtake you. We would later have a meeting and solidify this business deal. I was perplexed now by the report that the dear doctor was telling me. I pondered what this would mean for The Heart. I did not preoccupy myself with it either, but went about to do my Father's will in New Jersey.

The Same Virtue

We stayed in New Jersey for the duration of the conference. While we were at the continental breakfast in the hotel lobby, Minister Annette and I were sitting at our table, enjoying a relaxing moment, when an older lady approached us. She came over to our table and sat down, and began to prophesy to me. She assured me that everything was fine and I was not to take any thought regarding my wellbeing, for the Lord had taken care of everything. She went on to tell me of the great things that the Lord had in store for my church and me. It wasn't long into her speaking that I discerned the essence of who she was. I cried out, "Oh, my God the same virtue." I looked at her and for surety I knew her. Oh my God, again I said, "The same virtue."

Then I went on to explain to her that in 1987, while tutoring for the Upward Bound Program, I was on a ship in Charleston, South Carolina, when I encountered an angel. She looked at me. I went on to tell her the story about an older lady such as herself who had spoken to me on the ship about the bondage of fear, and that I would no longer confess fear. I told her the other lady, who I would later learn was an angel, gave me the exact same feeling I had in her presence. "Ma'am," I said, "her husband accompanied her just as your husband is accompanying you, but he spoke not a word. You are the same couple I saw in 1987 in Charleston, South

Carolina." She did not agree or disagree: she just listened to me. I said again with surety, "The same virtue."

Then I insisted that she write her address in my green address book. She did. Minister Annette and I both witnessed her writing their names and address. When I got home, I looked for the address, but could not find the address in my address book. The address had vanished. "God Talked," and confirmed that they were indeed the same angels. The older couple that I met in New Jersey at the hotel bore striking similarities to the couple I saw in Charleston, South Carolina in 1987 on the ship, who the Lord later told me were angels. This story is told in another "God Talk." The couple in New Jersey was from Charleston, South Carolina. This is not a coincidence, but again rather providence and God's way of a "God Talk."

Well, the time came to leave Bridgeton. I had done what the Lord required of me. There were so many who wanted me to come over to their house because they had heard of me through various family members who had moved to Georgia from New Jersey, and some were members of my church. One family had prepared me a feast. We were detained by that family until we almost missed our flight. We shared many "God Talks." We cried and we laughed, we rejoiced. Then we realized that so much time had passed, and if we didn't hurry to connect with Elder Dairsow and George, we would miss our flight, so we made haste.

We arrived at the airport. We were flying out of Philadelphia between 6:30 and 7:30 p.m. I was far more at ease because I had experienced flying and it wasn't so bad after all. It sure beat driving! I knew what to watch out for this time. I prayed earnestly that God would give us a beautiful blue sky. I thought as long as there were blue, clear skies, there would be no turbulence. It was evening and the horizon was golden orange arrayed with purple mist. It was absolutely breathtaking! It was take-off time. Once we were in the sky, I needed to go to the restroom. I was so full of peace and confidence. I asked where was the restroom. I saw a line of people waiting. Well, I would not escape the line. I got up and walked to the back of the plane and got in line. I was laughing at myself: I felt like an old veteran. I looked out the window and the plane seemed to rest in the clouds. *Wow,* I thought, *it looks like I'm walking in the sky on the clouds.* I was back to my seat in no time and they came with the cart. The sky grew darker and darker until it was night. Nightfall was a total new element that I had not factored in. I had a quick "God Talk." I had to check with God about this matter. Then I noticed it was cloudy and then the rain. *Oh Lord, we are going to experience turbulence.* I braced myself and waited for the dreaded bumping. Before I could bat an eye, we were descending into the nightline of the Atlanta sky, lit up with so many lights it looked almost like day. I felt the wheels hit the ground. We had landed and not one time did we experience turbulence. Praise God!

It sure felt good to be home. It seemed like an eternity that I had been away, although it was only about five days. I went back to work that Monday. I was in my office when I received a phone call from my sister. She was in shock! "Sabrina, Sabrina," she cried out. "Were you not just in Bridgeton, NJ? I told them you were there."

I was trying to make sense out of what she was saying. I needed her to calm down so I could make sense of what she was saying. She went on to tell me that some of our family had called from St. Petersburg, Florida, to tell us that my mom's first cousin, two children, and grandchild had been murdered. She said, "Tracy and Ronald Coleman, our cousins were shot to death by her boyfriend. Tracy's fifteen-year-old son was killed also. The boyfriend that did the killing committed suicide by hanging himself, and the only person that was not killed was Tracy's baby."

I gasped for air and became totally immobile. Oh, my God! My sister said, "I told them you were in the same city." I had not a clue that my mom's first cousin's kids were in the same city where I had just spent almost a whole week.

My heart ached as I thought of my mom's cousin's wife, Pumpkin. Their father, James, would bring them down to Georgia every summer to visit. We would hang out and go pick plums and have such fun in the summer. I remembered Tracy and I were close in age. We were very close when we were little girls. I remembered my cousin, James, their dad, looked like Lou Royce. Pumpkin was tall with a fair complexion, a very pretty lady. I always admired her hair. Oh, my heart grieved for my family, for Pumpkin. My cousin, James died years ago, leaving Pumpkin a widow. When he died, the trips to Georgia ceased. We lost contact with the family in Jersey, but the St. Petersburg crowd continued to make trips to Georgia. I was bewildered by the thought that I was in the same city and God had hidden it from me. It would have been so exciting to reunite with them, and now these unimaginable horrors — three family members murdered, and a little one was the only one who remained amidst a domestic violence dispute.

It was said that Tracy had just made a call to the authorities about 6:50 p.m., less than an hour before their murders. I pulled up the report online. It was reported that on Sunday, June 6, 2010 that at 7:30 p.m. on the 2700 block of Evergreen Court, multiple shoots were fired. Multiple gunshot wounds had killed each of them. I fell over on my desk and wept. All of this happened during the same hour I was leaving Bridgeton. "God Talked" and assured me, had I known they were in the city, I would have possibly been with them. All I knew was that God had kept me from ever knowing I was in the same city with such close relatives.

I would later learn through multiple phone calls how many members from my church knew them personally. They grew up with them in New Jersey. Their mom, Pumpkin, was a member of the Union Baptist Church where Mother Marie's home going was held. I had been in the same circle but had no knowledge that they were in the same city. Even Elder Dairsow knew my family. The child was all that was left. The message that God had given me for Bridgeton would become paramount for my family, a "God Talk," "Strengthen that which remains: There is still life in you." Tracy's baby would sure need strengthening. I had not a clue how far-reaching that message would be. Elder Dairsow offered to fly me back to New Jersey, but God did not give me leave due to spiritual fatigue. It was critical that I rest. It was heart-wrenching for everyone who persevered through this tragedy.

When I arrived home from New Jersey, there were bags and bags of clothing on my back steps. I had no idea who had left them, and then shortly after that batch there was again even more clothes left. This time there was a note from a very dear friend whose name I choose not to disclose. It read, "Sabrina, my husband died, I thought some of the members at your church could use the clothing." My heart dropped. He died while I was away in New Jersey. What could have possibly happened? He had left me a note before I went to New Jersey, telling me he was going to divorce his wife. I was shocked. They seemed to have a good solid marriage and were planning to retire.

I couldn't imagine what all this would mean for the church, because it was God using his wife that blessed us with the sale of the property. Now, he was dead. What possibly could have happened so fast? I called my friend to see how she was doing. I learned she had gone through so much that I will not disclose in this "God Talk." However, from the minute he gave me the note, God had me interceding for her. I know God placed her in my life. In fact, she is my very dear friend. I only tell this one to show how the "God Talk" uses the angels to bring me comfort in times of uncertainties regarding church property. She told me how he went in the hospital for a simple procedure and died. Needless to say, she was still his wife and whatever his intent was, it never came to fruition. They were still very much married when all this befell him. She assured me that everything was fine with the church and the contract guaranteed that the terms and conditions could not change, and that we would just need to make the payments to her. "God Talked," and everything regarding the property for the church was fine, and I had no need to concern myself any further. That's what the angel assured me of in New Jersey. "God Talked," and everything was fine!

Stop Trying to Work The Anointing: Let The Anointing Work For You

God continued to have "God Talks" with me through dreams. I had a dream where I was driving a car. The car veered out of control. I spoke in the dream and commanded the car to straighten up. It immediately did so, and I was amazed at the power. Then the car veered out of control again, and this time I continuously commanded the car to straighten up in the name of Jesus, but I did not get immediate results: This time it took some work, but eventually it straightened up again. Whew. I was relieved again and intrigued at the power of God. Then the car veered out of control again and went off into the ocean. The water so beautiful and clear swallowed my car. I was submerged in deep, clear blue water. It was so real that I could feel the coolness from the water, but no water got in my car.

I was in awe and "God Talked" and asked me, "What are you going to do now?" Then I woke up. I asked God, "What are you saying?" but He didn't answer me. On my way to work, as I made the turn on Phinizy Road, "God Talked." "Sabrina stop trying to work the anointing and let the anointing work for you." I pondered what all that meant for me. I was always working so hard. I am certain God wanted me to slow down, but I was confronted with so many obstacles like the water that my car was submerged in, I was submerged in trials and tribulations and everything in me was always fighting to stay afloat. I was dealing with some of the most trying times of my life. The words of my Momma Liza always rang in my head, "Sabrina, you better slow down or you are going to run right out of this life." Funny, my friend was always saying the same thing, but in a different way, "Girl, you would pass your shadow and wouldn't know it."

Father, Don't Let Her Say Another Word

I had filed a grievance for the first time in a twenty-two-year work history against my supervisor. I was so battle fatigued in this season. I really did not want to go through anything else. I was dealing with some serious issues with my sister and her wedding. The supervisor at work proceeded to come at me with a vengeance despite my every effort to keep peace. I considered not following through with my grievance until the Lord spoke to me through a dream and "God Talked." "Can the Ethiopian change his skin, the leopard his spots? Then may ye also do good, that are accustomed to do evil (Jeremiah 13:23)." I was at wit's end. One day I was walking at the back of my building and there was a called meeting with my supervisor. I just didn't know if I could bear anymore. I cried out a "God Talk," "Father, Father, don't let her say another word to me, Father, I don't want to dishonor You." That day I went on to the meeting and she sat directly next to me, but God honored that "God Talk," and she didn't open her mouth throughout the duration of the meeting. When the meeting was over, the one word she spoke was, "God bless you." Funny, how out of the mouths of some proceed blessing and cursing: Out of their mouth come sweet and bitter waters.

It would be weeks before she spoke anything else to me. I laughed at God. "I know I asked You not to let her speak to

me, but I just meant for the duration of the meeting." I told
God, "You could let her talk now." God gave me a message
during this season: "Don't let a fool distract you from your
purpose." Abigail was married to Nabal and Nabal was a fool.
His name means fool. Abigail interceded to stop King David
from killing Nabal by reminding David of his destiny for
the throne of Israel. David said he would have surely killed
Nabal had not God used Abigail. Abigail would later become
David's wife after the death of Nabal (1 Samuel 25:1-44).
God was reminding me of my destiny and that I had to continue to walk in love.

So much trouble in this season, and nothing was letting
up. I was indeed forging new weapons in my arsenal during
this season. Love was the greatest weapon of all against all
the attacks of the enemy. My love walk was being forged into
the fourth dimension of love, as described in Ephesian 3:17-
19, "That Christ may dwell in your hearts by faith; that ye,
being rooted and grounded in love, May be able to compre-
hend with all saints what is the breadth, and the length, and
the depth, and the height; And to know the love of Christ,
which passeth knowledge, that ye might be filled with all
the fullness of God." God was stretching me into the fourth
dimension of His love, and He would use my sister to test
me. Oh, it is often our loved ones that He tests us with. God
proved Himself strong in me during this season: He demonstrated His perfect love through the whole ordeal with my
sister from the cycle of sacrifices, being cursed and called
every foul name the devil could spew out, from threats and
lies and assault on my character, from weeping and crying to
almost breakdown from the treacherous dealing of the enemy
through my own sister, to a call for love that had to be walked
out and lived out. That is another story altogether, another
"God Talk."

Chapter Eleven

Forge

"God Talks"

"Behold I have created the smith that bloweth the coals
in the fire, and that bringeth forth an instrument for
his work: And I have created the waster to destroy, No
weapon that is formed against thee shall prosper and
every tongue that shall rise against thee in judgment thou
shalt condemn. This is the heritage of the servant of the
Lord, and their righteousness is of me, saith the Lord."
~Isaiah 54:16-17

Stir Up The Gifts

God always is faithful to give a Word in season to prophetically position His people for the upcoming year. The Word He spoke for 2010 was "forge." Initially, when "God Talked" and impressed this word in my spirit, I had not a clue as to where He was going with this word, but I knew it would prove significant for me and the people of God. He always confirms what He speaks. There was a mix-up with a purchase I had made the day before that proved not to be a mix up at all, but rather a setup for another 'God Talk." I was anxious about returning the items and getting the transaction corrected. I was on my way to return the item to the store when "God Talked." On my way, I passed New Century Homes – a mobile home dealer. They always had scriptures printed on their marquee. I was rushing so, that in passing I caught a glimpse of it but didn't recall reading it as I often did when I would pass by on my way to work.

I had made it a little past the Peach Orchard Road and Tobacco Road intersection when "God Talked" "Turn around and go back to New Century Home." I said "God, I am really in a hurry to get to the store to return this item, and not to mention I have a marriage counseling session at 1:00 p.m." Stopping at Century Homes was not in my plans, but God was up to something and I knew He had a plan and His superseded my plans. So, I did a swift u-turn and headed back to Century Homes.

When I arrived, I really didn't know what purpose God had designed for me to stop by there, so I walked in by faith. When I entered the office, I immediately felt the Spirit prompting me to ask for the owner. I walked in the first office and a young lady pointed to the main office. When I entered the owner's office, I greeted her and began to share with her how God had sent me by to encourage her. He told me that the business was a ministry and had ministered to so many people that passed by every morning, and no matter what she was experiencing in the business finances, she was to stay the course because He was with her to give her success and it was just a season till she would see God's salvation. She looked at me and her eyes were filled with tears. She expressed her gratitude at what the Lord had sent me by to tell her, and that they were experiencing a slow season. She rejoiced at the "God Talk," and she and I begin to share testimonies to the glory of God.

I shared with her how I couldn't but help noticing all the pecan trees they had on the property and how loaded those trees were. She went into a room and came out with a massive bag of pecans and said, "These are for you." She told me her daughter, Amy had picked the pecans up for her grandmother. I was so elated because I had just given my daddy all of my pecans. I remembered how "God Talked" and told me to give my daddy all of my pecans.

Anyone who knows me knows pecans have the value of gold to me. I just love my pecans. So it would take God to tell me to give all my pecans away before I would to do so. You sure can't beat God's giving, and obedience is truly better than sacrifice. God had given me abundantly more than I had given away. The owner of the business expressed to me how much I was like her daughter. She exclaimed to me, "You got to meet Amy." As Amy's mom and I were conversing, in walked Amy — tiny and petite but a fireball for Jesus Christ.

As she walked in, she fixed her eyes on me, and asked if she could pray for me. I found it a bit unusual because rarely if ever do I recall people wanting to pray for me. I was always praying for people. I had to gather my composure before I consented. I sure welcomed the opportunity to have someone pray for me, but I was sent there to do ministry and didn't understand that God had more in store than I had perceived. She said, "Before I pray for you, I have something–a gift that I have had riding around in my car since Christmas." This was the day before New Year's Eve. "That gift is for you and I want to give it to you." She ran out to her car to get the gift. When she came back in the building, she had this beautifully wrapped package with a whisk attached to it with a big red bow. She placed it in my hand and began to help me rip the gift paper off of it. It was a beautiful set of bowls with a large bowl-like platter. Anyone who knows me knows that I like to entertain and I love cooking and entertainment dishes for presentation. I still have it on my inspirational table.

She laid her hands on me and prayed affirmatively in a proclamation style, "You are a land of Goshen"…"Stir up the gifts"…"As the gifts are stirred up in you, they will be stirred up in those around you." As she prayed, she prophetically dramatized and proclaimed what God was doing for my life. I wept through the whole encounter. There I was sent to minister, and now God had someone ministering to me. I don't recall in all my life someone speaking in the manner that Amy spoke that day.

During the latter part of the year of '09, God was using me to engage in prophetic acts — in fact, He told me how He was restoring prophetic acts back to the Body of Christ and that I would see more and more of this ministry emerging on the time scene because it was part of the arsenal He was releasing to the church in the end times for warfare. I was so refreshed and "Stirred Up" — "God Talked." He supernaturally redeemed the time. I had just enough time to make it to my ministry appointment and not to mention He gave me success in getting my transaction right — Praise God!

Forge

The encounter with Amy at Century Homes would prove instrumental in further revelation concerning the word "forge." I continued to seek God on New Year's Eve to know what He was saying concerning "forge." **Webster's Dictionary** defines "forge" as a place where metals are heated and hammered. Also a secondary definition Webster offers is to advance gradually but firmly. Even as I am writing about this, "God Talked." The second definition struck deep to the core because I missed this part of the definition as I went through this season, which gives even more insight as to what I experienced in 2010. I waited on God for even more insight until the word resonated with me spiritually. God led me to Isaiah 54, and as I was reading, the fire leaped off the pages of scripture. "Behold, I have created the smith that bloweth the coals in the fire, and that bringeth forth and instrument for his work; and I have created the waster to destroy. No weapon that is formed against thee shall prosper, and every tongue that shall rise against thee in judgment thou shalt condemn. This is the heritage of the servants of the LORD, and their righteousness is of me, saith the LORD" (Isaiah 54:16-17).

"God Talked." He told me how in the upcoming year, 2010, He would forge new weaponry and that the level of warfare would intensify, therefore new strategies would be needed for the upcoming battles. He let me know that the demonic powers that would be unleashed in this season would require advancement in the knowledge of spiritual artillery. The amazing thing is that God further confirmed what He had spoken. "God Talked" that night when I got in from New Year's Eve services. I picked up my red prayer book and opened directly to page eighteen to the section, "Declaration for The Coming Storm" (Pastor John Kilpatrick). In that declaration, the very words that Amy spoke over me leaped off the page: "I decree, proclaim that this house shall be a 'Goshen': a place of safety, a place of security, a harbor of peace of rare abundance, and a house of more than enough, Your alms shall be remembered as a memorial before the Lord (Prayers, page 18)." Amy had decreed over me that I was a land of Goshen and that my ministry would refresh many. God continued to give progressive revelation. On January1, 2010, "God Talked" through yet another book, *The Great Controversy: The Coming Storm* by Ellen White. I picked the book up and opened to page 191, "The hearts of the disciples were stirred. Faith was kindled. They were 'begotten again unto a lively hope' even before Jesus revealed Himself to them." "God Talked" and there I was stirred and again enlivened with hope for the upcoming storm.

Ask For Your Family; You Won't Be Denied

I had just experienced so much in 2009. God's power was like fireworks on the Fourth of July that crescendo into greater levels of unceasing awe until the finality and "Glory to God." I will recount some of the "God Talks" that happened in 2009.

One Wednesday after noonday prayer with one of my prayer warrior partners, "God Talked" and told me to call my daddy. The tug at my spirit alerted me that it was urgent. I recall the way the Spirit led Pastor Evelyn and me to pray that day for miracles of healing – the word miracles stood out more than any other word that I could recall. It was still sounding off in my spirit when the Lord urged me to call my dad. I had spoken with my dad that Sunday and he was in the hospital–from 2008 through 2009, my dad had faced constant challenges of illness and prolonged hospitalizations, but his unwavering faith in the Lord Jesus had sustained him. He had by this time faced being a double amputee, both of his legs having been amputated. Now he was confronted with the challenge of kidney failure and having to receive dialysis all at the same time, while staying the course of his ministry as a pastor of New Bethel Missionary Baptist Church in Fort Lauderdale, Florida. I had assumed he was released Monday and was home doing fine. I called my dad the following Wednesday and to my surprise he was in a crisis. I could hear the sheer panic of my stepmother through the phone lines as she frantically asked me to call back in about fifteen minutes. Anyone ever faced with something of this nature knows that those fifteen minutes can seem like eternity. When I did dial them back, my daddy answered the phone and he said, "Pray for me." I said, "Daddy, I will pray for you," and he said urgently, "Pray Now." At the moment, I lifted my face toward heaven and made intercession for my dad as never before. After I prayed, he calmed and I asked him if he needed me to come to Miami. For the first time in all my forty-plus years, my dad said he needed me to come. He had never made such a request of me, and I knew the urgency of the hour. He had been through so much but never required that I get to Miami in a hurry. I held to the "God Talk" about miracles. The peace of God will keep you miraculously during such times. I was calm and finished up at work that day and let my supervisor know that I had to go to Miami to see about my dad.

I went to Bible study that night and I informed my congregation about what had transpired that day and that I would be leaving for Miami the next day. That night was so amazing at Bible study. The church air conditioning had gone out, and instead of canceling our Bible study, we did Bible study on the church front lawn. There was so much peace in the atmosphere. I had such assurance. God had given me two messages prior to all of this that prepared me for everything. One was about Rahab the harlot, which was "You can ask for your family." Rahab asked not only for her life but also for her family's life in Joshua 2:12-21. Then He gave me another message "You won't be denied," about Zolephehad's daughters who asked for their inheritance even though it was not permissible by law for women to inherit. Nevertheless, they went before Moses and the council and asked for their father's inheritance because he had no sons. When Moses inquired of God, God did not deny them, and the law was changed – rewritten, giving them the right to inherit as told in Numbers 27. God had given me these two "God Talks" for the season I was now facing.

My Aunt Virginia traveled with my son and me. The Heart of Jesus Church Family was very supportive and would stand in the gap as intercessors as we made the trip. We departed Thursday as we had planned. When we arrived, sure enough, my dad was in ICU and was gravely ill. When we entered his hospital room and walked over to his bed, he rose up and grabbed me and pulled me to his chest almost in a headlock and exclaimed with exuberant joy how glad he was to see me. He was hooked up to all kinds of machines and all his equipment was beeping. I had never seen my dad like this. My step-mom explained what was going on with him, and things didn't look promising. We were in for a week or more of constantly being at the hospital.

While we were in Florida at the hospital with my dad on the first day, I received a phone call from Minister Annette and Deacon Otis Johnson that attended my church; they were in route to New Orleans. Minister Annette's brother, Brother Anderson Brihm Jr. who was traveling with them who didn't attend my church got on the phone, and said, "Pastor, the Lord said you would not be denied." This was a "God Talk" moment indeed! He didn't have a clue of the messages that God had given me weeks ago in preparation for this season. I knew God would honor my request for my dad's life.

We would often have long waits in the ICU waiting room as they were doing different procedures on my dad. During those times, I would often seize the opportunity to minister to others who were very distressed as to what was going on with their loved ones. There were several cases where God used me to intercede. There was one lady who was in quarantine? She had the dreaded swine flu, which had literally become an epidemic and was making headlines. She was very critical and was not expected to make it. She had to have an emergency C-section to deliver her baby as a result of her illness. The baby was on another floor in critical condition. Her family was from Georgia as well. In fact, they were from Wadley, Ga., where some of the members of my church lived. Small world. As we shared, we learned that they even knew some of the same people we did. I went to her ICU room with their permission so I could pray for her. I stood on the outside of the room and laid my hands on the room door and cried out to God for her life and her baby's life. I had full confidence that God would save her and her baby alive. I consoled the family with words of faith.

There was another family of a young man who had an aneurism and had a violent motorcycle crash. He had suffered multiple injuries to the spine and severe brain damage. His prognosis was very bleak. His aunt was a schoolteacher, and she said to me as I encouraged the family that sometimes God says no. I responded to her, "But this time He will say yes." Then there were two other families. One was a young lady who had a stroke and she was on life support. Her room was next to my dad's room. Her family allowed me to come in and pray with her. Again, I encouraged the family to believe God. Then there was another young man on the other side of my dad's room who was in violent car crash and he was on life support as well and declared brain dead. I prayed for him as well.

In the meantime, my dad started asking for his brother and sisters to come from Georgia to Miami. He was acting as if he believed he was not going to make it. So all my aunts and my uncle, along with my cousin, made an emergency trip to Miami as well. We all stayed at my sister's house.

They were all anxious to get to the hospital to see my dad. They knew something was dreadfully wrong because my dad had never made such a request. It was like he wanted to see everyone because he suspected that he would not make it this time. My sister was crying. She shared with me how God had given our dad more years. She shared with me how my dad had been diagnosed with bone cancer during the same time our mom had cancer and died in 1993, and it was so far gone that there was no medical intervention offered. My dad prayed and turned his face to the wall and cried out to God, and God granted him more years.

It was 2009 and my dad had done absolutely fine, to the astonishment of his doctors and everyone who knew of the crisis. Amazingly, he had concealed this from the rest of the family. She cried the more vehemently, "God has granted Daddy more years already." My response to that was then He would just have to grant him more years. He did it before and He could do it again. While I was showering to get dressed to go to the hospital with my family, I cried out in the shower to God, "Father, Father, Father." The peace of God fell on me. I got out of the shower and my sister was still crying. I told her to quiet herself, because God had not shown me death and I was certain daddy was not going to die, and if he was going to die, then God would have shown me. God and I were very good friends.

We left to go to the hospital to take our family who had come at my dad's request. When we arrived, my dad was doing amazingly well. He was talking to everyone, sitting up, and even had a burst of laughter. He shared how he had seen the color blue with such intensity and otherworldliness that he could not describe. He shared how he thought he was leaving us, but there he sat, totally vibrant and full of life. Everyone was overwhelmed and relieved when they saw him. We took countless family photos. It was truly miraculous. His condition continued to improve. In the meantime, I went about to check on all the others I had been praying for. The young lady with the swine flu was miraculously better, and her baby also. The young man with the aneurism was up and talking — they were even talking about rehab for him. The young lady with the stroke was off life support and the young man who had the car accident was improving. I shared all the reports with my dad and family. All of this happened in just a few days of my back and forth to the hospital. My dad exclaimed, "The Lord has truly walked through this place."

My family who came down returned to Georgia, but my aunt, my son and I stayed. They moved my dad out of ICU to a regular floor. The room they moved him to was a very long room that he shared with a Hispanic middle-aged man. If you were on my dad's side, you would never know someone else was even in the room, that was how much they were separated. We were thanking God for all He had done for so many families in the ICU. God moved so miraculously, until I thought for a moment He would close the ICU unit down.

One day while we were leaving my dad's room, the Hispanic gentleman frantically grabbed my hand as I walked by his bedside. "Ma'am, will you pray for me?" I turned and immediately I began to intercede on his behalf. What was amazing was that my aunt walked by him, my sister walked by him, my stepmom walked by him, even my son, but he grabbed my hand and cried out, "Pray for me, Ma'am. Will you pray for me?"

After I finished praying for him, I shared with him that I was a pastor from Georgia and my church name was The Heart of Jesus Church. He was so relieved that I had prayed for him. He constantly kissed my hand and could not stop saying thank you. I knew in my spirit that God had honored his faith. I was not sure because he did not discuss it with me, but I couldn't help but believe he overheard some of the testimonies of the others who were miraculously healed.

Perhaps he did: I do not know. What was so peculiar was how he picked me out of everyone who passed.

The next day when we returned to the hospital, his doctor saw my aunt when she entered my dad's room. She said his doctor stopped her and inquired, "Who was the lady that prayed for my patient?" My aunt said that she told him it was her niece who was also her pastor. The doctor told her, "Please thank her for praying for my patient," and reported how he had a total turn around and was doing so well that he was about to be discharged. My aunt assured him that she would give me the report.

My dad was doing so much better that I shared with him how we were planning to leave. We had been in Miami for almost two weeks. The look on his face showed me that he was not ready for us to go. He asked me to stay a little while longer. He shared with me that he wanted me to go to church with him that Sunday. He was discharged from the hospital that Friday. We stayed until Sunday as he had requested. Unbelievably, despite his health crisis, he was determined to go to church that Sunday morning. He mustered up the strength and we all went to church. I recall when we arrived; the side entrance door was locked. He banged on the door and one of the members of the church opened the door and gasped in sheer joy, as if she had seen a ghost. She exclaimed, "Rev. Lewis." The gazes of everyone in the church fell on my dad, seemingly shocked because they were not expecting him.

My dad grabbed my hand and I assisted him to the pulpit and he turned and beckoned for me to stay. My dad stood up at the podium to address his congregation. He started out by telling them he had been wrong about women in ministry. He expressed how he had always believed that it would be one of his sons who followed in his footsteps of ministry, but instead God chose one of his daughters. He then announced to his congregation, " Today she shall bring the message." I almost fell through the floor: I was totally awed! "Look at Jesus."

What a moment. I could barely move my feet, they seemed to be glued to the pulpit. God used me mightily that day at my dad's church. Many people flooded the altar for prayer. I was still frozen in the moment of my daddy not only recognizing my ministry, but allowing God to use me at his church, which became one of the most prized moments of my life.

About three years after this "God Talk," my good friend, Rev. Christopher Johnson would later ask me to speak at an Interfaith Coalition on Gender Inclusion. He specifically asked me to share the testimony about my dad. Dr. Joseph Lowery, the dean of the Civil Rights Movement, was the keynote speaker at the event. I was flattered when he commented on my speech and I actually gained greater insight into other reasons my dad opposed me. Dr. Lawry said, "Young lady, I think you might be a little hard on your dad, my daddy didn't believe I was called to preach either, and I am not a woman." He went on to tell a story of how his mom told his daddy that God had called him to preach. He shared how one day his dad showed up where he was preaching and after hearing him, his daddy proclaimed to his mom "By God, God done call that boy to preach." He shared how he was very moved by my testimony and that he just wouldn't believe in this day and age that women were still being opposed in ministry. The truth of the matter is that in some sectors they are.

One thing I understood about my dad's opposition that day was that he really was seeking to protect me from the hurt that comes along with pastoring. One of the things I shared with the Interfaith Coalition was that when a person is in a crisis, it doesn't matter who prays for them. It doesn't matter whether it is a woman or a man, black or white, Jew or Gentile; all that person needs is intercession — someone who can get a breakthrough for his or her life. "The Lord will perfect that which concerneth me: thy mercy, O LORD, endureth forever: forsake not the works of thine own hands" (Psalm 138:8).

God continued to talk through this "God Talk." My dad was well enough to make his annual Christmas trip to Georgia. During his stay, he preached at my church. He was strong and courageous as he shared his testimony of the ordeal he had suffered. He amazingly can quote passages from all the Psalms. He starts at Psalm 1 and goes through every Psalm quoting a passage. My church was always intrigued as to how he could do that. He often explained to me he had lived every one of them and they were ingrained in his life. He had an unwavering resolve to continue in ministry, never retreating from the challenges he often faced as a double amputee, and now after this last crisis as a dialysis patient. He gave God all the praise as he shared his testimony. Sheer joy could be seen on his face as he lovingly attested to the faithfulness of God. The whole church stood as he gave his testimony.

Then just a week later, after my dad had left to go back to Miami, I would get one of the biggest surprises ever. I had shared with my congregation all the miracles God wrought when I was in Miami. I especially had shared the account of the Hispanic gentleman. While I was teaching Sunday school the following week, the Hispanic gentleman burst through the front entrance of the church with such excitement. "Ma'am, ma'am, remember me, you prayed for me, ma'am. How is your daddy?' He fell on my neck and embraced me in tears – we were both crying. In fact, the whole congregation was in tears. "Ma'am, I am well and I brought you a gift and your church a gift." A gentleman friend accompanied him who remembered me also from the hospital. He had traveled all the way from Miami to visit a friend in Augusta and he expressed how he was determined to find me. All he knew was the name of my church, The Heart of Jesus Church.

"God Talked" through situations and circumstances. He orchestrates events in our lives that will speak to us throughout eternity. He granted me the reward of seeing the labor of my "God Talks." An answer to my "God Talk" stood right before everyone in the congregation that day. They all had heard the story, and now God was talking to everyone as they witnessed the gentleman who came all the way from Miami and found a small church in the middle of the country, just to come and show gratitude for what God had done for him. He left his number with me, but I lost it and eventually we lost contact, but I could never forget this "God Talk."

Chapter Twelve

"Give Place"

"God Talks

"He said unto them, Give place: for the maid is not dead,
but sleepeth. And they laugh Him to scorn. But when
the people were put forth, he went in, and took her by
the hand, and the maid arose. And the fame
hereof went abroad into all that land."
~ Mark 9:24-26

My House Sits On a Hill

I had yet another dream. This time the dream setting was at twilight. I looked outside from my front door to see that it was flooding. There was another house that sat very close to my house. I noticed the water was running down from the side of my house as some water had settled around my house, and the water around the house was about ankle deep. The water was so crystal clear — pure, clean running water. I could see the grains of sand glistening like gold dust under the water. I looked at the beautiful water that was pooling around in a continuous circular motion. I stared in amazement when all of a sudden; the water began to flow up the hill. I knew in the dream that that was supernatural movement: I said to myself, "Water doesn't flow up a hill." I turned away from the front door and went to the bathroom. Suddenly a baby girl appeared in my arms. I was washing and caring for her. I was cleaning her because she was soiled. As I was cleaning her, I heard a frantic knock at my front door. So, I turned and went to the door and there stood my neighbor yelling, "You got to get out of the house, it's flooding." I protested, "No, my house sits on a hill, don't you see — my house is on a hill." I closed my door and went back to taking care of my baby.

Now that I am writing about the dream, it had two elements. One of the elements was dimness and yet one of refreshment. I know the baby was my church. One thing I was certain of was that my house was on a hill. I would be kept from the impending danger, but I was also being warned.

Make Room For The Miraculous Move of God

Only be a week or two later, I was on my way to work. I had to drop my son off at Augusta Tech before I went to work. I had noticed the night before at Wednesday night Bible study I experienced an unusual pain in my ear that seemed as if it was pulling my inner ear out of my head. It was so painful, I shared with my congregants who were at Bible study that I had a pain in my ear, but I was resisting. Well, throughout that night, I appeared to be all right. In fact, one of my members, Ann, was in a spiritual crisis and I prayed and warred against the witchcraft spiritual attack she was under. She experienced total deliverance that night and magnified God for what He had done. She repeatedly cried, "Thank God for you, pastor."

I noticed when I was en route to take Dee to school, I felt slightly dizzy. By the time I made it to work, I was increasingly dizzier. I was staggering and I was nauseated. I sat at my desk for a brief moment, trying to get my composure. I noticed I was feeling sick. I prayed and resisted. I called my boss and friend, Linda, to let her know that I might have to go home because I was feeling sick. After I hung up with her, I had to run to the bathroom to regurgitate. I started regurgitating profusely — projectile. This would go on for some time. I became more off-balance, staggering all over the place. My co-workers were alarmed and very concerned. Liz and Jennifer continued to ask if I was okay. It was apparent that I wasn't. I called my sister to pick me up because I knew I was unable to drive. I had called Dr. Rassekh's office and they said that I could come on in and they would work me in. My sister assisted me to her car and took me directly to the doctor's office.

When we arrived at the doctor, I was barely able to walk and I continued profusely regurgitating. I was over in a corner away from everyone. I noticed my sister Brenda was walking back and forth, trying to see if they could take me on back. Instead they asked her if she would take me home and bring me back at 1:00 p.m. I could tell Brenda was a little upset with the way the receptionist was acting. She struggled to get me to her house and up a flight of stairs. Brenda lived on the second floor of the apartment complex. I continued to profusely regurgitate. I tried to lie down in between the episodes of regurgitating. I regurgitated so much until all I was bringing up was clear lime green liquid. I felt faint. Brenda came to the room where I was lying down to let me know it was time to go to the doctor. It was such a struggle to get up, but we managed. When we walked out into the cold air, it seemed to revive me some. I was very hot.

When we arrived at the doctor, Brenda had to take care of everything for me. Then we were in the back, waiting on my doctor. All I could do was lie almost motionless. Dr. Rassekh entered with his nurse. He looked in my ear and I heard him tell my sister that he was afraid that my eardrum would rupture. They gave me a shot for the vertigo, and some amoxicillin for my ear and Claritin D. He sent me home, but I continued to get worse. My sisters, Karen and Brenda were trying to get me to eat some soup to take my medicine, but I couldn't hold anything down. I was growing weaker. Finally, later on that night, I heard "God Talk" and He told me that I was going to have to go to the emergency room. Shortly after that, I felt like I was passing out and then some kind of fluid began to run out of my ear. I was totally soaked from sweating.

I whispered to Brenda to call 911, that I needed to go to the hospital and I knew it was too dangerous for them to try to drive me. She called 911. It wouldn't be long before the paramedics arrived. They assured her that they couldn't bring the stretcher up to the second floor. I don't remember much, but they assisted me down the stairs and then put me on the stretcher. I could remember one of the attendants was a tall, fair-skinned man. I remembered them asking what hospital I wanted to be taken to and I heard "God Talk" and said Doctors. He was taking my vitals and asking me questions. I could remember him saying, "Stay with me, Ms. Lewis." I apparently passed out.

I don't remember arriving at Doctors Hospital. I didn't know anything. My sisters tell me I was fighting them because I was trying to get up and go somewhere. They said they couldn't hold me and that I was swinging them around like rag dolls. Brenda said the only thing that seemed to calm me was when she got in my face and screamed, "Pastor Sabrina Lewis." Then she said I fell back in the bed and calmed down. I must have been in and out of consciousness. I remember someone trying to force me to do some MRI. I fought for my dear life. I remember some huge nurse forcing her weight on me — pressing me down. I felt like I was suffocating. "Get off of me," I protested. I fought so much that they abandoned their efforts to do the test. I don't remember anything after that. I believe all day Saturday I must have been in a coma-type state. My family reported that they let me fall out of bed when they first admitted me to ICU, and because of that they put me in restraints to keep me from injuring myself. I was unaware of any of this.

The doctors informed my family, church family and friends that I was a very sick woman and that they feared I had meningitis and things really didn't look good for me at all. They shared with them how I might not make it. Pastor Joyce and the others said the doctor's reports were very negative, but she said God reminded her of the promise for my ministry of the 1,500 souls that He would give to The Heart of Jesus Church. God gave me this promise for souls that would come to the church. She said they all went to the chapel in the hospital to have a "God Talk." Everyone was requesting that other prayer warriors they knew pray for me also. They tell me there were so many people at the hospital on my behalf, and at least two people stayed around the clock for five days.

I vaguely remember Sunday evening, waking up slightly. I was so hungry. I saw some familiar faces. I really didn't realize what had happened to me. I was looking around but everything was strange and unfamiliar. I had so many people coming back in the ICU room to see me. I could make out some of them at times and at times I couldn't. I remembered my son. He just sat rubbing my head. He said I was mumbling something, but he didn't understand me. Others shared with me how hard this was on my son and that he just couldn't take it. This would go on for five days. I was very critical. They wanted to move me to MCG Trauma, but I was too sick to move. They said the risk was too great, so they had to do whatever they were going to do where I was. They also said that I needed emergency surgery on my ear. I think my son gave consent for one of my surgeries. My sugars were off the chart; my blood pressure readings were off the chart. They told me when my eardrum ruptured that the pressure was like an explosion in my head: It ripped a hole in my eardrum and the infection had got up in my brain. They had me on multiple strong antibiotics.

It would be a day-by-day report and they were not making anyone any promises. They said that this was very rare. I had a team of at least six doctors. I finally was coherent enough for them to do a MRI and a CAT scan with contrast. They felt like I might have suffered irreversible damage. Amazingly, I remembered telling my doctor on about the fourth day of my stay about my job. I told him I was a work therapist and that I worked with mental health consumers and forensic consumers. Dr. Lindman was amazed. He shared with me how they thought that I would not make it and my surviving was a miracle. He said to me, "Much prayer and this little tube I put in your ear saved your life." I looked at what he held in his hand and I couldn't believe it what I was seeing; He held in his hand a tiny little plastic tube no bigger than a centimeter in diameter and width. They assured me that I had a long road to recovery once I was out of the woods. I was in the critical care ICU Unit for five days and I was moved to the Step Down ICU Unit for the next seven days. I spent a total of twelve days in ICU.

Dr. Rassekh called my sister on several occasions. Brenda was furious with them. She said during my first few days they called her several times, apologizing for what happened at the doctor's office. They said they wanted to know how I was doing. She said, "You all sent her home twice and now she is in ICU fighting for her life." She said they continued to tell her how sorry they were to hear what had happened. Needless to say, many of my friends were angry and felt that my doctor was responsible for my crisis and should have sent me on to the emergency room. I was finally doing somewhat better and they moved me to the Step Down ICU Unit. I was still very dizzy and off balance. My vision was very blurred and I could barely see because my diabetes sugars were running very high and I was on ten blood pressure medications. Prior to the crisis, I was only on one blood pressure medication and I was not insulin dependent. I just took two Glipizide pills a day. I could only sit up and walk for very short periods. Most times I would lie down. I felt like I was in a space zone. I told Dr. Lindman that I lost my sense of normality. I did not know what normal was anymore: Everything felt strange. I continued to try to connect with reality. I felt almost schizophrenic. I continued to call on the name of the Lord. I constantly thanked God for my life, but I never perceived death — I knew I would live through this. Remember, "My house sits on a hill."

My friend, Alexis had given me a healing CD and a CD on The Generals. I listened to the healing CD night and day. She said "God Talked," and told her to come every single day to visit me. She wasn't aware of the nurse director's request that my visitors be limited because I had absolutely too many visitors and she felt I needed to rest. I didn't agree with her assessment because what I really needed was my family and friends, because they were the only ones who helped me make a connection with reality. My friend, Julie didn't leave until I was out of the Critical Care ICU. She had traveled to Augusta from Macon, Georgia. I continued to have many visitors.

My favorite pastime was reading God's Word, but I couldn't because for the longest time I couldn't see. I would try to read and get very frustrated because I couldn't until "God Talked," and said, "Rest." When you are used to going so much, it is hard to stop and just rest. In this instance, God didn't leave the choice to me: I couldn't do anything but rest for days.

They started my therapy in the hospital. They started walking me out of my room some. When I would walk, my head would seem to be like a bobbing head and I would get totally nauseated and fatigued. Even four years later as I write this, I still live with these symptoms on a daily bases. Some days my symptoms are intense and some days not as intense, but always there! In fact, writing this "God Talk" has proved the most difficult. I was so overwhelmed by writing this "God Talk" until my whole system shut down. What I try to avoid the most is total shut down, because at that point I find even basic life duties almost impossible to perform — something as simple as taking a bath and getting dressed. It sometimes takes hours before I recuperate. So I relentlessly try to engage myself to avoid getting that far gone. I had to abandon writing yesterday. My sister, Teresa, who has helped me with this writing project, witnessed the meltdown. I thank God that through many "God Talks," He has strengthened me to resume.

Someone brought me some reading glasses and that was the best gift ever. I could read. God always talked to me as I would read. I so desperately wanted to hear what He would say in regard to my crisis. I had a bag of my books along with my Bible, my most treasured possessions. Even my ability to read was compromised because I could only read for short durations before I would become fatigued, but how I rejoiced for just the brief moments I could read. As I was reading *Prayer in Another Dimension*, by Sue Curran, "God Talked." "Make room for the miraculous move of God!" "God Talked," "He said unto them, Give place for the maid is not dead, but sleepeth. And they laughed him to scorn (Matthew (9:24)." God assured me death was never in the plan, this had happened for His glory, and to give a place for Him to work miracles. In other words, I would have to trust that He would work this for my good no matter how tragic it seemed at the moment. Peace filled my heart to submit to the process of this season. Up until this point, I was struggling with it.

It all happened so fast. I went to work December 2, 2010 with never a thought of the events that would unfold that day. I was trying to make sense of it all at first, but after this "God Talk," I let go!

The coming season would prove very challenging. I had the "God Talk" to "Give Place" to hold on to. I just wanted to go home. After twelve days in the hospital, I was being released. My sister, Brenda came to pick me up. I was so excited about finally going home. I was sick of the hospital food. It all tasted like grass. No disrespect to their food: I am certain it was all the massive amounts of antibiotics and other medicines. Everything tasted like grass. My sister tried to convince me to go home with her, but I insisted that I needed to go home. Home, the word itself sounded so warm and inviting. If I could just get home, everything would fall in place. It was the first time since my hospital stay that I had been outside. Air, cold crisp air, it felt so good! I got in her car and it seemed like I was riding in a spacecraft: The ride home was excruciating. I thought for a moment Brenda would have to stop and maybe we needed to do a little at a time. "I am sick! Oh, God, please get me home." It seemed like an eternity, but she pulled up in my yard. She could barely stop the car before I was out of it, going up my steps, wobbling all over the place. I just felt if I got in my house, I would feel connected — normal.

I walked into my house with a great sigh of relief, but only to discover that though my surroundings were familiar, I didn't feel normal. My house felt like I was in space. Oh just let me get in my bed. I got in my bed and I had a spinning episode. The reality hit me that I was very much still sick. Brenda stayed with me for a whole week. She watched every move I made. Day by day, I tried to gain some sense of normal.

I would battle with the basic activities of daily living. I dared not go outside. My world in my 1,977-square-foot mobile home was proving to be more of a world than I could handle. Then one day I tried walking outside and my system really shut down. The outside stimuli would prove too much for my vestibular system. After many doctor visits and long sessions of rehabilitation, I was told that my right ear was completely wiped out — all my hearing and my vestibular system. I went to countless specialists, neurologists and all. The final word was: nothing further could be done medically. My inability to hear out of my right ear and the total compromise of my vestibular system made some simple tasks of daily living into threatening events. There was the constant threat of falling during simple maneuvers in my home. One day while I was going to my mailbox, I was almost hit by a car. It scared me so bad. The problem was that when I was walking, I would avoid turning my head from side to side because my symptoms would escalate.

I greatly appreciated everyone driving me everywhere, but I longed to drive myself. It would be about two months before I could drive and even then with extreme precautions. I learned one thing: I could drive better than I could walk. My therapist explained to me that when I was walking, my system was more challenged because the brain was working to keep me upright and then perform the activity I was trying to engage in as well, but when I was driving my system only had to work at the task. She assured me it wasn't strange at all, but they often observed this to be true for other patients.

I had to do vestibular exercises daily. I always had assignments from my therapy sessions that were meant to challenge my system. After months of therapy, they determined that they had done all they could do and I was not much better. Dr. Lindman referred me to Dr. McKinnon at MCG. He was said to be the absolute best doctor for what I was experiencing. There was so much going on, so much of my life came to a halt. I couldn't return to my job where I had worked for over twenty-two years. My time was running out, and then my short-term disability would run out. The state of Georgia allowed donated leave: I received so much time from my co-workers that they had to send out an announcement asking people not to donate me any more time and I had to return time back to people. They said this was highly unusual. My livelihood was threatened, medical bills, other bills. It would be months before I could handle any of my business. By the time I attempted to do so, everything was so overdue. I wanted to get back to my church. After all, I was the pastor.

I remember a "God Talk" where I reminded God that He would always give me a Word for the upcoming year. 2010 proved to be "Forge." He told me 2011 would be, "Give place for the Miraculous Move of God." In the midst of shambles, God worked miracles. There would be periods where He provided miraculously for me. My beautiful members would give of their time, talents, and treasure. I am speechless when I think about how they all stood with me through this season. They modeled the Heart of Jesus! God allowed me to preach December 31, 2010, but it would be a while before I would preach again. I could only partially resume some of my pastorate, and extremely limited at first. The one thing I could do was test and engage myself. If I couldn't, I didn't, and I didn't have to. It would have been a very different case on my job. I worked with mental health and forensic consumers. I missed them terribly, but in this season I could only focus on regaining some of my life.

I recalled that I even looked funny because my eyes would do strange movement when I walked. My therapist told me that I was balancing myself with my eyes. I remember that one of the first things I wanted to do was go to Goodwill. I did and I was totally wiped out because it was too much to look through the racks. I had to sit down. Even now shopping can be challenging. My worst nightmare would be a visit to Walmart – especially the Super Walmart. One day I had to call my cousin Sabrina to come get me. Even now I have to limit my shopping. Parking decks and garages are also a nightmare for me.

Expedite The Process

The hardest thing for me to admit would be that I was disabled. This was the most dreaded word, but I was. I would go through a second rehab where it was determined again that I had maxed out and vestibular rehabilitation would not benefit me any further. One day "God Talked" when I got to Dr. McKinnon's office, and told me to ask him about disability retirement from the state. He was determined to get me better and the subject had never come up, but when "God Talked" I asked. He immediately turned to me and said, "What are we waiting on? Let's do it." I got the retirement packet from my job and turned it in to him. Typically, this process could take weeks.

I gave him my package, which was more than forty pages long, on a Friday. That Monday morning when I got up, during a "God Talk," God led me to ask Him to expedite the process. Before I could get off my knees, my phone was ringing and it was Dr. McKinnon's office. The receptionist said, "Miss Lewis, we have your packet ready." Unreal! I made haste to go pick it up. My packet was submitted to the State of Georgia November 16, 2011. They informed me that the process would take at least six months. "God Talked" and gave me the word for 2012 as the year of completion. I had seen many miracles during 2011.

One day when I checked my account and all my donated leave had run out and there was no check deposited, I cried and had a "God Talk" that Friday morning. When I got to church that Sunday, Pastor Joyce and Minister Frieda expressed to me how they had been praying for my finances. Before church was over, one of the members of the Heart – a young brother by the name of Mike — walked up to me and put a thick roll of money in my hand and hugged me and said God had told him to give me what he put in my hand. Pastor Joyce and Minister Frieda were so excited they pulled me to the office and counted the money in my hand. It was $1400. The Wednesday following that, my spiritual mom, Dot walked into noonday prayer and put an envelope in my purse with $1000. Before the week was over, I had been given more than $3,000, twice the amount of what my bi-weekly check was.

Due to the fact that I had been off-payroll, I had to pay all of my benefits out-of-pocket. I had to make choices. I gave up my vision and dental insurance, but I had to maintain my health insurance because of my medical crisis, which was very expensive without a paycheck. That money carried me for a minute and then a need arose again. This time "God Talked," and instructed me to asked my friend to loan me $500. She loaned me the money until whenever I could pay it back. Then there would be yet another time and "God Talked" and told me to call my friend, Pastor Dwayne, who dropped a check off to my house for $700. Then as the year drew to a close and I still had not received any news, I needed more money. I preached during Watch Night Service how God said 2012 would be the year of completion. I received a letter in mid-January from the State of Georgia. My retirement was effective 1/1/2012. "God Talked," it was complete. The letter stated the amount I would receive every month and gave me the opportunity to change my retirement option before my first check. It stated that once I received the first check, I could not change my option. I noticed the error of my option. I had asked for accelerated benefit, which would give me a higher yield at first and then after the first five years would level off. I knew "God Talked" and had assured me that was the option for me. I made some phone calls and faxed a letter to make sure I had the accelerated option.

Everything was corrected, but I still would not receive my check until the end of the month. "God Talked" and told me to go to my home town bank — First National — and request the amount of money I needed to pay my bills for the rest of the month and have money for food and other necessities. I went to my bank, and all I had to show them for income was the letter stating my approval for retirement. All the medical bills had dropped my credit score from 670 to 423. I cried because there was yet another thing this crisis had done to me. I remembered one day at Goodwill, "God Talked" and gave me a book that was titled, ***The Crisis that you thought would take you out: Would be the Crisis that would bring you in.*** Well, my banker Clifford Lewis approved the loan before they checked the credit score and they assured me it had no bearing on my approval, but they had to check it because of bank policy. Clifford and I shared testimonies that day of how God had kept us both through our crisis.

"God Talked." I would have never imagined my life would have taken such an abrupt turn. When people would say, "You're getting closer to retirement," I would always say, "I don't know what the Lord would do." He could do anything! Here I was at the end of a "God Talk," retired from my job. God brought back to me how, about a year before all this happened, during a "God Talk" when I was fretting about the crisis I was having with the boss who was harassing me, He said to me, "I could bring you off the job." Now here it was a "God Talk" complete!

To purchase additional copies of this book,
you may contact Pastor Sabrina Lewis at by email at
pastorsabrina7@yahoo.com

CPSIA information can be obtained
at www.ICGtesting.com
Printed in the USA
LVHW081439230822
726675LV00023B/207